UNIVERSITY OF WISCONS
IN
THE SOCIAL SCIENCES AN
NUMBER 25

THE GENOSSENSCHAFT-THEORY OF OTTO VON GIERKE

A Study in Political Thought

BY

JOHN D. LEWIS

ASSISTANT PROFESSOR OF
POLITICAL SCIENCE
OBERLIN COLLEGE

MADISON

1935

CONTENTS

PREFACE

The publication of this study gives me a welcome opportunity to record my obligations to all who have in any way assisted in its preparation.

For their courteous permission to use the portions of Gierke's works included in the Appendix, I am grateful to the following German publishers: to the Weidmannsche Buchhandlung, for the selections from *Das deutsche Genossenschaftsrecht;* to M. and H. Marcus, for the chapter from *Johannes Althusius und die Entwicklung der naturrechtlichen Staatstheorien;* to Duncker and Humblot, for *Das Wesen der menschlichen Verbände;* and to J. C. B. Mohr (Paul Siebeck) for the passages from *Die Grundbegriffe des Staatsrechts und die neuesten Staatsrechtstheorien.* I wish also to acknowledge the kindness of the Yale University Press in permitting the use of quotations from the works of Harold Laski and from Rupert Emerson's *State and Sovereignty in Modern Germany.*

To the Institute of International Education, I owe the opportunity of a year's study at the University of Berlin from 1932-1933, when the material for this study was gathered. Among many helpful experiences of that year, I am particularly glad to recall the kindness of Professor Julius von Gierke, Otto von Gierke's son, professor of jurisprudence at the University of Göttingen, to whom I am indebted for a very pleasant and illuminating conversation about his father's work and thought.

For constantly valuable advice and criticism at various stages of the work, my deep thanks are due to Professor John M. Gaus of the University of Wisconsin. I also wish to thank Professor Oscar Jászi and Professor Karl F. Geiser of Oberlin College and Professor Frederic A. Ogg and Dr. Llewellyn Pfankuchen of the University of Wisconsin, who read and criticized the completed manuscript.

My gratitude to Dr. Ewart Lewis need not be expressed here.

Some mention should be made at this time of Ernest Barker's recent translation of a section of Volume IV of Gierke's *Das deutsche Genossenschaftsrecht,* which he entitles *Natural Law and the Theory of Society, 1500-1800;* this did not appear until after the completion of the present study. There is also in existence a translation of Gierke's *Johannes Althusius* . . . , by Dr. Bernard Freyd, which we may hope to see in print soon.

JOHN D. LEWIS.

The University of Wisconsin,
    November, 1934.

INTRODUCTION

I present this study of Gierke's association-theory[1] as a partial answer to questions about Gierke which I had often encountered but never found satisfactorily explained. Since the publication in 1900 of Maitland's translation of a brief section of Gierke's *Genossenschaftsrecht,* Gierke's name has been frequently cited by American and English jurists and political writers. But until very recently English-speaking writers have been content to take their interpretation of Gierke from Maitland's introduction and to refer vaguely to the four ponderous volumes of the *Genossenschaftsrecht.*[2] While I do not wish to imply criticism of Maitland's brilliant introduction, I do think it very important to point out that Maitland was interested primarily in the private-law implications of Gierke's theory. When writers use Maitland's Gierke in support of public-law and political theories, the use challenges examination. The necessity for an examination of Gierke's general political theory which might serve as a basis for judging the validity of appeals to the authority of Gierke on the part of both radicals and conservatives was the first motive for this study.

The second motive was more specific. It was the desire to discover what bearing Gierke's association-theory might have upon the theory of federalism. I should state at once that I do not use the term *federalism* in a strictly juristic sense. I do not use the term in reference exclusively to relations between a central state and member states. I use it rather to denote a principle of organization as applicable within non-state groups and between political and non-political groups as between central and member states.

---

[1] I use this phrase as the most convenient, if not entirely satisfactory, translation of the German *Genossenschaftstheorie,* because the general term *association* seems to me preferable to Maitland's too colorful *fellowship.* In many cases, however, it has seemed to me better for the sake of clarity to leave the German *Genossenschaft* untranslated.

[2] Only recently there has appeared a study of Gierke by a young scholar from the London School of Economics: Sobei Mogi, *Otto von Gierke, His Political Teaching and Jurisprudence* (1932). The study is open to much serious criticism. The section on Gierke in Rupert Emerson, *State and Sovereignty in modern Germany* (1928), although very brief, presents a much more accurate and balanced interpretation. See also F. W. Coker, *Organismic Theories of the State,* in *Columbia Studies in History, Economics and Public Law,* vol. 38 (1910), pp. 76-80.

It is difficult to find a precise definition for the principle of federalism. The following approaches it:

> Federalism . . . in its most general sense is a principle which . . . is characterized by a tendency to substitute coördinating for subordinating relationships or at least to restrict the latter as much as possible; to replace compulsion from above with reciprocity, understanding, and adjustment, command with persuasion, and force with law. The basic aspect of federalism is pluralistic, its fundamental tendency is harmonization, and its regulative principle is solidarity.[3]

The statement that American federalism, in theory as in practice, has developed in an atmosphere of extreme individualism is no longer to be regarded as a startlingly novel observation. The influence of the natural-law theorists upon colonial and revolutionary American thinkers has long been recognized; and the impact upon receptive American minds of ideas popularized by such writers as Grotius, Pufendorf, Milton, Locke, and Blackstone has been subjected recently to revealing study by American scholars.[4]

Judicious selections from the writings of Locke and Milton, and even from the conventional and conservative Blackstone, furnished useful ammunition for the final protest on a natural rights basis against England. Human equality, natural rights, the social contract, strict limitations upon governmental action, the right to revolt, played a determining role in both propaganda for complete separation and the rationalization of the decision. As early as 1765 Samuel Adams summarized the case against England in these words:

> 1) *Resolved,* That there are certain essential rights of the British constitution of government, which are founded in the law of God and nature, and are the common rights of mankind;—therefore
>
> 2) *Resolved,* That the inhabitants of this Province are inalienably entitled to those essential rights in common with all men: and that no law of society can, consistent with the law of God and nature, divest them of those rights. . . .[5]

---

[3] Max H. Boehm, "Federalism," in *Encyclopedia of the Social Sciences*, VI, p. 169.
[4] *Cf.* Carl Becker, *The Declaration of Independence* (1922); Benjamin F. Wright, Jr., *American Interpretations of Natural Law* (1931); Charles G. Haines, *The Revival of Natural Law Concepts* (1930).
[5] Resolutions adopted by the House of Representatives of Massachusetts on March 29, 1765, cited by Wright, *op. cit.*, p. 72.

And a year later the same appeal was clearly expressed in a pamphlet by John Dickinson:

> Kings or parliaments could not *give* the *rights essential* to happiness .... We claim them from a higher source— from the King of Kings and Lord of all the Earth. ... They are created in us by the decrees of Providence, which establish the laws of our nature. They are born with us; and cannot be taken from us by any human power, without taking our lives.[6]

The most vigorous and effective appeal to natural law and natural rights came, of course, from Thomas Paine. "Man did not enter into society to become *worse* than he was before, nor to have fewer rights than he had before, but to have those rights better secured," he tells us. "Every civil right has for its foundation some natural right preëxisting in the individual. . . . Society *grants* him nothing. Every man is a proprietor in society and draws on the capital as a matter of right."[7]

The classic piece of documentary evidence on the practical influence of the natural rights philosophy is, of course, the *Declaration of Independence*. In the second paragraph of the *Declaration* the "self-evident" implications of the philosophy are developed with a conciseness and force difficult to match in the whole literature of natural law. The evidence is amplified by the inclusion in almost all of the early State constitutions of a bill of rights, usually preceded by a philosophic preamble echoing the language of the *Declaration*.

The work of the practical-minded American "fathers" may be considered a reaction against the philosophic radicalism of revolutionary thinkers like Samuel Adams, Paine, and Jefferson. Men like Jefferson and Gerry, suspicious of the degree of power to be given the new government, returned once more to natural rights for support of their demand for a safeguarding bill of rights.[8] But the task of the convention was not to proclaim attractive general principles. It was the task of creating a workable organization which would reconcile and protect the divergent interests of dominant groups. In lieu of the purely national system favored by some, but obviously impossible, the convention created a strongly

---

[6] *Address to the Committee of Correspondence in Barbados* (1766), Wright, *op. cit.*, pp. 77-78.
[7] *The Rights of Man*, in *Writings* (ed. Conway), II, pp. 306-307.
[8] *Cf.* Wright, *op. cit.*, Ch. VI.

centralized system of federalism based upon a definite and permanent contractual relation between the states.[9] It could not, however, suppress philosophic principles which armed the opposition for assault upon the rights of its labor. But it could, and did, construct a system which might be depended upon to control and modify the implications of those principles for the assurance of safety and stability. Moreover, even the most conservative of the members found it possible by skillful logic to turn the guns of their critics back upon the critics themselves.[10]

The controversy of the period of the revolution and convention was, with the exception of some phases of the slavery controversy, the single occasion for a thoroughgoing philosophic consideration of the fundamental principles of political society. Principles adopted, developed, and popularized for specific purposes—principles upon which both conservative Federalists and radical Republicans were able to build popular appeals because those principles were so readily taken for granted—have continued as axiomatic fundamentals and have gathered around themselves an almost irresistible emotional appeal. The atomistic individualism of the natural rights philosophy has been further bolstered and popularized by the impact upon American thought and character of the frontier. Even before the work of Frederick Turner and the elaboration of his thesis by enthusiastic disciples, the significance of the frontier was generally recognized by historians in its most spectacular form of "Jacksonian Democracy"—an aggressively equalitarian and individualistic democracy which makes the cultured, philosophic radicalism of Jefferson look a little pale.

The spirit of atomistic individualism, born of the natural law philosophy and toughened by a continual struggle with the challenge of the frontier, has remained to a remarkable degree the dominant spirit of American social thought. "The assumptions of 1789 have, with rare exceptions, continued to be the assumptions of the twentieth century," Wright tells us.[11] Court decisions, learned articles, the effective shibboleths of party platforms and political speeches amply justify his opinion. This uniquely American spirit of individualism—in so far as it can be analyzed—is a

---

[9] Cf. Charles A. Beard, *An Economic Interpretation of the Constitution of the United States* (1913); Beard, *Rise of American Civilization*, Vol. I, Ch. VIII; Max Farrand, ed., *Records of the Federal Convention* (1911).
[10] Cf. James Madison in the *Federalist*, no. 48 and no. 51.
[11] Wright, *op. cit.*, p. 149.

spirit which tends always to formulate social problems in terms of an antithesis between two social entities, the individual and the state (or, as it is sometimes stated, the individual and society); which tends to think of the state (or organized society) as an organization of convenience based upon contractual relations between isolated individuals; which all too readily assumes a perpetual conflict between the two entities; which seeks, therefore, to preserve a balance by a strict recognition and distribution of rights, powers, functions between the two social entities and then among the divisions of the governmental organization.

From this point of view every novel extension of social control, regardless of its necessity, becomes an "encroachment" upon the "sacred rights of the individual." Examples are innumerable; but nowhere has the battle for individualism been more consistently and stubbornly fought than in the Supreme Court. Regulation of hours of labor is found to interfere with the right of contract and therefore to deprive the individual of part of his liberty.[12] The prescription of a minimum wage for women deprives employer and employee of the right of free contract and is an insulting implication that a woman is less able than a man to protect her own interests.[13] "Yellow-dog contracts" become a legally-protected recognition of liberty of contract.[14] It is unnecessary to reproduce here further evidence so generally known.

The ideas so carefully and elaborately expressed by the judges and scientifically reworked by scholars like William Sumner and even the German-trained J. W. Burgess have found less judicious but more popular expression at the hands of influential leaders. President Hoover was very fond of contrasting "the American system of rugged individualism" with "European doctrines of paternalism and state socialism." The acceptance of the latter, he told us, "would have meant the destruction of self-government through centralization of government. It would have meant the undermining of the individual initiative and enterprise through which our people have grown to unparalleled greatness."[15] Mr. J. M. Beck has repeatedly expressed extreme concern over the disappearance of the individual among the wheels of federal bureau-

---

[12] *Lochner vs. New York.* 198 *U.S.* 45 (1905).
[13] *Adkins vs. Children's Hospital,* 261 *U.S.* 525 (1923).
[14] *Coppage vs. Kansas,* 236 *U.S.* 1 (1915); *Adair vs. U.S.,* 208 *U.S.* 161 (1907).
[15] New York *Times,* 23 October, 1928, p. 2, cited by J. Mark Jacobson, *The Development of American Political Thought* (1932), p. 513.

cracy. He demands that the increasing expansion of governmental control be checked in order "to maintain in the scales of justice a true equilibrium between the rights of government and the rights of an individual." In the spirit of the Constitution, he seeks to defend "the integrity of the human soul."[16] Mr. E. H. Gary finds his way clear back to Paine when he tells us that that government which governs least governs best.[17] One can imagine the eighteenth century revolutionist shuddering with horror could he meet his modern disciples and realize the reactionary implications in the twentieth century of the revolutionary principles of the eighteenth.

Within this general framework of negative individualism there has been an unavoidable tendency to formulate the American theory of federalism in terms equally atomistic, mechanical, rigid. The practical assumption, suggested in the *Federalist* and expanded by Madison, that the new constitution *divided* sovereignty between the federal government and state governments did not prevent repeated appeals, beginning as early as 1792, to state sovereignty or states' rights, as one state or group of states after another found itself in opposition to particular policies of the federal government. *Chisholm vs. Georgia,* the Kentucky and Virginia Resolutions, the threats of secession by Massachusetts and Connecticut in 1811, the Nullification Ordinance of South Carolina prepared the soil for Civil War arguments. Although Calhoun repudiated the natural law philosophy, his arguments, based upon the claim that the states alone were sovereign, that the union was a mere compact among sovereign, independent states, hence that nullification was justifiable, were almost a duplication upon a higher level of the natural law arguments of the revolution. The replies of Webster and Story were the replies of constitutional lawyers who assumed, or pretended to assume, that the whole argument was one to be settled by narrowly legalistic interpretation of the contract of union.

Again it is to states' rights, whether "natural" or constitutional, that those turn who are moved by an honest fear of over-centralization or by reactionary dislike of socially desirable regulation. Federal control of corporations engaged in interstate trade, indirect federal control of intrastate carriers, adequate regulation of

[16] J. M. Beck, *The Constitution of the United States* (1924), p. 206.
[17] Cited by Jacobson at p. 511 from Beale ed. of H. Spencer, *The Man versus the State,* p. 72.

child labor, the preservation of natural resources—each new attempt to meet the challenge of a completely transformed national economic and social structure must face the powerful opposition of interested groups and honest but short-sighted individuals armed to the teeth with arguments which have become part of the American political tradition. A United States Senator feels that the acceptance of the child labor amendment would mean "a complete surrender of most essential reserved powers of the states," and bitterly suggests that the amendment, if successful, might well be followed up by an amendment abolishing state government entirely.[18]   Governor Ritchie tells us that the system of federal grants in aid "strikes at the very heart of American institutions and destroys the American theory of local self-government."[19] On another occasion Governor Ritchie solemnly warns us against the paternalism, the materialism, the tyranny which accompany· "governmental interference with the rights of the states and with the rights and immunities of the individual in the states."[20] Such protests and warnings come not only from occasional senators and governors, but from a large and influential group of political leaders, among whom we find such men as President Taft, President Coolidge, President Hoover, Nicholas Murray Butler, and Governor Moore of New Jersey. The language they speak is popular and convincing because its vocabulary and style are rooted so firmly in American sentiment. But it is language which helps to blink facts, avoid practical problems, and conceal reason in clouds of emotion.

Whether the philosophy of the "New Deal" involves a departure from traditional American ideology—as numerous enemies and some friends of the Roosevelt program insist—is, it seems to me, impossible to determine from such close range. But we do begin to find today writers who, antedating depression and "New Deal" in their revolt against this traditional American spirit of negative, atomistic individualism, are looking for a way of expressing in understandable terms the obvious fact that political society is something *more* than a group of isolated individuals artificially bound together by mechanical legal relationships.   Miss

[18] Duncan Fletcher (Florida), *North American Review*, CCXX. (1924), pp. 238-244.
[19] Address at the Annual Convention of the Pennsylvania State Chamber of Commerce, Harrisburg, Pa., 15 October, 1925; cited by L. T. Beman, *States Rights* (1926), p. 296.
[20] Address at the Boston City Club, cited by Beman, *op. cit.*, p. 335.

Follett[21] and John Dewey,[22] starting with the pluralistic[23] concept of social life as a complex pattern of interest or functional groups, have attempted cautiously to move on from there to a theoretical expression of the necessary organic integration within the complete pattern, and have suggested an ideological approach towards the factual realization of such integration. We must cease to think in terms of isolated individuals, they tell us. We must cease to think of political problems in terms of conflict between individual and state or state and state. We must learn to look below the surface of constitutional divisions of power and mechanically legal organizations of individuals; we must learn to recognize the interdependence of individual and individual within intimate and more remote groups, the mutual reaction upon each other of individual and group, the reality and significance of group life, the necessity of ordering the relations of group with group, of the individual with his groups, by principles capable of integrating without solidifying the social structure.

This reaction against mechanical individualism, while it is natural and, in the writer's opinion, desirable, is not without its own danger. At the opposite pole of political thought from individualism we meet a tendency which, in various degrees of intensity and clarity, has directed the thought and permeated the theories of innumerable writers from Plato to Hegel and his followers. It is the tendency to think of society, and particularly of political society, as an organic rather than a mechanical, contractual entity. Leading almost inevitably towards theories of extreme unitary centralization, this organic approach has been regarded legitimately with suspicion by Americans and Englishmen. Its nationalist, ultraconservative results appear in the political theory of Hegel and some of his German followers whom I shall discuss later.

In turning to Gierke I have gone deliberately in search of a compromise approach for contemporary political thought which might avoid at the same time the evils of a negative, mechanical individualism of the sort which has dominated American political thought and of a reactionary, mystical statism of the sort which still dominates much of German political thought. Is such a com-

---

[21] *The New State* (1918); *Creative Experience* (1924).
[22] *The Public and Its Problems* (1927).
[23] I do not mean to suggest that either of these writers is a "pluralist." Their point of departure, however, is very close to that of the pluralists.

promise to be found in Gierke's *Genossenschaftstheorie?* That is my first question. Does the *Genossenschaftstheorie* offer a basis for a theory of federalism more adequate to present-day needs than the individualistic, social-contract basis which still seems to prevail in the United States? That is my second question. To avoid misunderstanding, I must stress the warning that my study is purely theoretical. I make no attempt to apply tentative conclusions or suggestions to practical problems of federalism, presentation of which at this point could only be superficial. Nor do I attempt to do more than present as accurately and clearly as I can my own interpretation of Gierke's position and the implications of that position.

CHAPTER I

That social theories do not grow in vacuums is an axiom no longer in need of proof. We realize that ideas can not simply be lifted from one political, social, ideological context, and, set down in a quite different context, appear either reasonable or intelligible. In reading Gierke it is particularly necessary to keep in mind a number of broad influences which color his whole thought. To forget or to disregard these influences with the particular color they impart to his ideas is to misinterpret Gierke—as writers from opposite extremes of political thought have frequently done.

The first and most obvious warning to one who would understand and properly evaluate Gierke is that he was a Germanist, a determined, fighting Germanist. He began his work in a period still dominated in jurisprudence by the strict Romanist school of Savigny. To drive out the Roman invader became a mission which inspired his best work. Like the Romanists, the Germanists were very mindful of history; but their historical research took them back not to the Roman Empire, the Digest and the Reception, but along the path marked out by Grimm, to the law and custom of the ancient German Mark and *Gemeinde,* to feudal records, to town charters, to the rules of an endless variety of gilds and "fellowships." To get at what was really German in the law of Germany and to combat the influence of the new Romanist systematizers of the nineteenth century, the Germanists had to go back beyond the fifteenth century and even in that remote territory were denied the support of the "learned" jurisprudence already "romanized." Tracing through those principles of the law which were truly German was, of course, but half the task of the Germanists. Insisting upon recognition in practice of Germanic principles—attempting to restore a purely Germanic common law—was the second half of their task, and a part of the task which they took most seriously.

17

From the beginning of his academic career Gierke was a staunch Germanist. At the University of Berlin, where he took his doctor's degree in 1860, he came under the influence of Georg Beseler, who had already sketched in rough outline and included in his teaching the idea of a purely German *Genossenschaftstheorie.* From Beseler Gierke inherited the task of broadening the foundation for a German theory of associations by a thorough and minute study of the historical development of the German *Genossenschaft.* The first volume of the *Genossenschaftsrecht,* published in 1868, and dedicated to Beseler, was the first brilliant step in the fulfillment of the task which, pursued diligently throughout most of Gierke's life, had still to be abandoned, not quite completed, with the publication of Volume IV in 1913.

His enthusiastic Germanism sometimes carries him to a point which makes the reader wonder whether he too is not being swept away by the poetic ardor of the writer. A section of the introduction to Volume I of *Das deutsche Genossenschaftsrecht* is the best illustration.

> It seems almost as if this people alone were designated to create states which are at the same time united and free. . . . Inferior to no other people in their bent towards universality and in their capacity for political organization, superior to most in their love of freedom, the Germans above all others have a gift through which they have invested the idea of freedom with a special significance . . . this is the gift of organizing associations. . . . The vigorous progress of our own day . . . permits us to hope that the latest among the unified European states will be the most perfect. And that force which distinguished the Germanic peoples from the beginning of history and arose again victoriously out of every ominous change—the creative force of association— is more living and active in the German people of today than in any other people.[1]

Opportunity to direct his enthusiasm towards a definite and immediate objective came in 1888 with the publication of the first draft of the new Civil Law Code. The first draft of the *Bürgerliches Gesetzbuch* with its almost total neglect of the academic progress made by Germanistic jurists was both a bitter disappointment and a challenge to the Germanists. Gierke's old master, Beseler, himself took up the attack against adoption of the draft and encouraged Gierke to write a series of critical articles for

---

[1] *Das deutsche Genossenschaftsrecht,* I, pp. 3-4.

Schmoller's *Jahrbuch*.[2] These articles were followed in 1889 by an attempt to point out the improvements which could and should have been made.[3] The failure of the Germanists to modify the spirit of the *Bürgerliches Gesetzbuch* before its final adoption did not silence Gierke nor kill his zeal.

> And yet whatever may confront us, it is only cowardice that would give up the struggle for a worthy goal because one battle was lost or because the hope of victory had moved a step further away. The struggle for German law can not and will not die so long as there is a German people. If the *Corpus Juris* was not able to crush out German law, neither will a civil-law code be able to strike the death blow.[4]

He went to work promptly on the second significant task of his life, an attempt to analyze and interpret the new code on a broad, Germanistic basis. The first volume of the *Deutsches Privatrecht* (1895) was followed by a second volume on *Sachenrecht* in 1905, and a third on *Das Recht der Schuldverhältnisse* in 1917. "He felt himself obliged," declares Professor Stutz, "to save of the German law and for the German law what could still be saved."[5]

I am not competent to judge the influence in practice of Gierke's interpretation of the Code. But that is not the important point here. I wish only to point out the intensity and sincerity of Gierke's belief that a common German law really existed, that the principles of the imported Roman code, alien to the German spirit, must gradually give way to resurrected Germanic principles, that progress in German law could come only by clinging to deep-rooted Germanic traditions, and that the fight for German law was not a mere academic squabble but a serious, self-imposed duty. "That law is the product of the spirit of the people was for him an article of faith."[6]

From what has been said above, one would expect to find that much of Gierke's effort went into historical research. Being a staunch Germanist, he had also to be a serious and profound historian. Had he stopped with the first volume of *Das deutsche Genossenschaftsrecht* his reputation could have rested safely upon

---

[2] (Schmoller's) *Jahrbuch für Gesetzgebung, Verwaltung und Volkswirtschaft*, XII (1888); XIII (1889).
[3] *Der Entwurf eines bürgerlichen Gesetzbuches* . . . (1889).
[4] *Deutsches Privatrecht* (1895), Vorwort, p. vi.
[5] Ulrich Stutz, "Zur Erinnerung an Otto von Gierke. Gedächnisrede vor der Juristischen Gesellschaft zu Berlin," in *Zeitschrift der Savigny-Stiftung (Germanische Abteilung)*, Vol. XLIII (1922), p. xxxvii.
[6] *Ibid.*, p. xxxi.

the evidence there of painstaking thoroughness and dependable accuracy which combined with acuteness of perception and breadth of vision to make his productive scholarship. But he continued the same type of work for another half century, turning out, in addition to *Das deutsche Genossenschaftsrecht,* such an admirable model of scholarly study and literary skill as *Johannes Althusius* . . . .

But Gierke's historical research was of a special type—of that type best exemplified among English writers in Maitland. Both were historians; but both were also jurists. Both were interested in the past only, or at least chiefly, in so far as it could throw light upon the present. For Gierke particularly historical research is always the basis for his dogmatic jurisprudence; and dogmatic principles are always firmly rooted in historical tradition, in "the soul of the People." His position and method are well described by Professor Stutz:

> With slight modification what he once said of Gneist may be applied to him: not that part of the past which has been lived, but that part of the past which still lives is his concern. Therefore he opposed the separation of legal history and existing law, whether the separation was on the basis of subjects or of persons. Of a purely historical German private law he would hear nothing, and he demanded that every educated jurist, or at least every Germanist, busy himself not only in history but also in the dogmatic principles of the prevailing law. . . . He was one of the most comprehensive and brilliant thinkers of our day. But he always worked out from the certain and well-circumscribed sphere of his field of research—which, however, included the whole past and the whole present of German private and public law.[7]

In the introduction to the last volume of *Das deutsche Genossen-schaftsrecht* Gierke regrets that it will now be impossible to execute his original plan, which was "to erect upon an historical basis a dogmatic structure in which the prevailing German law of the *Genossenschaft* should stand forth as one whole."[8]

If Gierke's historical approach had the virtue of keeping his theory closely bound to fact and tradition, it also showed occasionally what many might consider the weakness of encouraging too deep a respect for existing institutions. Like Burke, Gierke was very willing to criticize and was very attentive to ideas for

[7] *Ibid.,* pp. xxxi-xxxii.
[8] *Das deutsche Genossenschaftsrecht,* IV, p. xi.

reform; but, like Burke, he could tolerate no criticism of fundamental institutions. The institution of the monarchy was one of these fundamentals; Prussian dominance in the Reich, historically proven to be necessary, was another; state sovereignty was a third; and, whatever havoc they might raise with his dogmatic system, still they had to be included.

A third important factor in Gierke's background was his reaction against the juristic formalism which had reached a point in Germany more extreme by far than the Austinian formalism which dominated much of English jurisprudence. In the attempt to create a true science of jurisprudence an important group of German jurists of the second half of the nineteenth century, led by Carl Friedrich von Gerber and Paul Laband, had broken with early philosophic and historical schools and tried to establish a "realistic" and "pure" jurisprudence unpolluted by social or political theory. They worked diligently at the task of skillfully sharpening concepts to a thin edge—only to cleave the thin air with their tools. The endless and pointless arguments over the juristic construction of the Bismarckian *Reich* are but an example of the results of this new formalism.[9]

Gierke realized the danger inherent in a loosely-used philosophic or historical approach—the danger of coming out of a confusing maze of material with vague, symbolic formulae or "mere juristic meditations." He admitted that "transparent clarity of concept is the noble goal of every science."[10] But his demand for realism and systematic thought could not be satisfied by the empty *Begriffsrealismus* of the formalists. His opinion of them could be expressed in decisive and rather biting language.

> The danger in this tendency lies in the fact that it considers the duty of science fulfilled when the dry material is in some way or other brought into a coherent system of logical categories. If the concepts be diluted thereby into empty and shallow forms, the thinness is transparent, the shallowness is intelligible, the formality sharply defined, and thus the desired clarity is achieved. Behind the formal solution the unsolved puzzle of real existence may swell up as mightily as ever. . . . If at numerous places the flood of life breaks through the artificial dam which the system has built up against it in its arrangement of categories

---

[9] *Cf.* von Ihering's parody upon this tendency: "Im juristischen Begriffshimmel," in *Scherz und Ernst in der Jurisprudenz*, (1885).

[10] "Die Grundbegriffe des Staatsrecht und die neuesten Staatsrechtstheorien," in *Zeitschrift für die gesammte Staatswissenschaft*, XXX (1874), p. 153.

> and sub-categories, the blame lies with the facts and not with the
> system. If research discovers hitherto unknown forces, if quite new in-
> stitutions appear, the formalistic approach . . . devotes the most care-
> ful and painstaking labor simply to reworking the new facts, formulat-
> ing and classifying them in order to squeeze them into the old formal
> structure and so be "through" with them without disturbing the closed
> system of concepts.[11]

> The jurist turns with justifiable annoyance away from all vagueness,
> darkness, confusion; he finds profundity and mysticism uncomfortable;
> what does not lend itself to definition does not exist for him.[12]

Against such legalism and formalism Gierke's substantial historical background was the best defense. His method of study
made him well aware of the larger pattern of social relations in
which political, economic, ethical factors were intertwined with
purely legal, and made him suspicious of all attempts to tear out of
the pattern artificially isolated concepts of abstract purity. "The
best proof of the soundness and utility of juristic abstractions,"
he tells us, "lies in their correlation with economics and ethics."[13]
And his idea of the pertinence to legal research of material not
strictly legal is well stated in the first volume of *Das deutsche
Genossenschaftsrecht:*

> Along with the legal side of the *Genossenschaft,* the cultural-historical,
> the economic, the social, the ethical sides certainly can not be disre-
> garded. They will, then, always be given so much consideration as is
> necessary for an understanding of the process of legal development or
> for demonstration of the inseparable interdependence which exists be-
> tween the system of law and the general cultural system.[14]

Gierke was himself a systematizer and a dogmatist; but his system had to grow out of the rich historical and sociological background which alone could give it life.

We must consider next a number of external influences upon
Gierke's work whose interaction with the factors noted above can
not accurately be measured, but whose general significance can
not be disregarded if we are really to understand Gierke. Born
in 1841, the son of a Prussian official who became Minister of
Agriculture in 1848 and President of the Court of Appeals at
Bromberg in 1850, later cared for by an uncle who was also a

[11] *Ibid.*, p. 154.
[12] *Ibid.*, p. 157.
[13] *Ibid.*, p. 160.
[14] *Das deutsche Genossenschaftsrecht*, I, p. 4.

Prussian judicial officer, Gierke spent his first years in an atmosphere highly respectable, sincerely patriotic, and intensely Prussian. The more important part of his university training he received at Berlin, where the spirit of Hegel and his followers was not yet dead, and where conservative Prussians still formed a center of opposition against the liberalism of 1848. In 1866 his study was interrupted by the call to arms. He served as a lieutenant of artillery at the battle of Königgrätz, and returned to the field again in 1871, winning in the second war the distinction of the iron cross. In the crisis of July, 1870, he shared the excitement of the loyal crowd *Unter den Linden,* as they awaited the outbreak of war; and many years later he spoke in poetic language of the deep impression the event left with him.[15] In 1914, an old man loaded with all the honors his profession had to offer him. he turned his mind and prestige once more to the defense of the fatherland. His speeches and articles during the war stand as evidence of a fervent patriotism which had grown with the years into an almost unquestioning faith in God, Kaiser, and Country.[16] He made his last important public address in May, 1919, on *"Der germanische Staatsgedanke."* Parts of this address are pathetic, even when read today. Looking over the chaos left by war and revolution, seeing the "shameless disavowal of earlier national spirit," "the rejection by the masses of all thought of their fatherland," the passing of the "age of heroes," he recalls the glories of earlier periods, then remarks sadly, "And today all that must be dead, and forgotten, and buried forever."[17]

An historical method of study leads always to a cautious conservatism in drawing conclusions. With Gierke this caution is heightened into a profound conservatism and his Germanism is made into an ardent nationalism by the events of his life which I have suggested briefly above. To quote once more from Professor Stutz' excellent sketch:

> His whole development and his historical-juristic habit of thought
> lead him more and more out of the milieu of the liberalism of forty-
> eight and into the camp of the conservatives. . . . "With God for

---

[15] *Das Wesen der menschlichen Verbände* (1902), p. 24.
[16] *Cf.,* e.g., "Krieg und Kultur," speech delivered 18 September, 1914, published in *Deutsche Reden in Schwerer Zeit,* No. 2 (1914); "Der deutsche Volksgeist im Kriege." in *Der deutsche Krieg,* No. 46 (1915).
[17] *"Und heute soll das alles vergessen, gestorben, für immer begraben sein!"* *Der germanische Staatsgedanke,* lecture delivered 4 May, 1919, published in *Staat, Recht und Volk,* No. 5 (1919), p. 24.

King and Country" remains even after the catastrophe his watchword.
. . . Prussian-German he was to the marrow. Not in vain had he heard
as teachers men who had fought for German freedom in 1813, not in
vain had he himself with the weapons of the soldier and those of the
thinker aided the rise of the dearly beloved fatherland whose age of
glory he had then watched throughout half a century.[18]

Remembering all this, it is not a little amusing when one of
Harold Laski's young followers, stressing but one side of Gierke's
political theory, claims him as a "pluralist";[19] and speaks of Hugo
Preuss as his true follower.[20] The same writer is much more accurate in his judgment when he speaks of Gierke as "a man of
1871."[21] There lies one of the most helpful keys to the understanding of Gierke. A Germanist, an historian, a realist, he was
also a staunch Prussian, proud of the Bismarckian *Reich*—and the
last attribute unified and intensified all the rest.

One last attribute of Gierke's personality demands attention.
Gierke always saw his problem with a quick, vivid imagination.
He wandered through masses of detailed materials, but he did not
lose himself because his way was always charted in broad and bold
outline. His subject is always alive and his problem dramatic. He
sees a modern idea growing out of the clash of fundamentally opposed principles traceable in detail through centuries of development. The clash becomes intensely real and the development intelligible to the reader because Gierke himself does not lose sight of
the first clear vision. A frequently cited paragraph from Volume I
of *Das deutsche Genossenschaftsrecht* is the best illustration of
my point.

As the forward march of world-history is inevitably realized, there
appears in an unbroken ascending arch the noble structure of those organic associations which, in ever greater and more comprehensive circles, bring into tangible form and reality the interdependence of all
human existence, unity in its multi-colored variations. From marriage, the highest of those associations which do not outlast their
members, grow forth in abundant gradations families, races, tribes and
clans, *Gemeinde*, states and leagues of states; and for this development
one can imagine no other limit than when, some time in the distant
future, all mankind shall be drawn together into a single organized

---

[18] Stutz, *op. cit.*, p. xxx.
[19] Mogi, *Otto von Gierke, His Political Teaching and Jurisprudence*, p. 120.
[20] *Ibid.*, p. 234.
[21] *Ibid.*, p. 267.

community, which shall visibly demonstrate that all are but members of one great whole.[22]

This is not the language of the usual scientific legal historian. It is the language of a scholar who is also a poet. It is a poetic imagination that works an otherwise unmanageable wealth of material into a unified whole. And it is poetic language which lends charm and conviction to generalities which differently expressed might sound inexcusably banal. Read as an example some of his discussion of methodology:

> On the other side, out of the consciousness of how narrow and inadequate are the concepts at hand, of how they cling to the surface, of how little they penetrate in their abstract, logical justification of form to the nature of the thing itself, there arises a tendency which bores into the depths. But the danger in this approach lies in the fact that in the unfathomed deep rests formlessness, confusion, darkness. All too often the bold diver brings to light, instead of the richly-suggestive concept which he hoped to create down below, only a notion, suggestive to be sure, but cloudy and confused. He strives in vain for a plastic formulation of the notion, and finally only achieves a more or less fantastic picture. . . . Intoxicated . . . by a glance into the mystic deep, the human spirit often lacks that conscious and energetic self-limitation which alone leads to certain mastery of the mind over material. Seeing change all about, it forgets the strict, logical following of conclusions; looking upon an unbroken chain of the past, it loses sight of theoretical bounds. The horizon seems suddenly to be infinitely widened; but ever more confused, formless, capricious become the mental images, ever more violently the flood of material rises over the shore, as chaos breaks upon the spiritual world.[23]

All this may be interesting, you will say, but scarcely relevant to such a study as this. I believe that it is quite relevant. It is good to remember that Gierke so frequently speaks in this poetic, slightly mystical language, for it is a language which by over-statement or over-colored statement invites misinterpretation. Gierke can be made a pluralist, a radical reformer, a reactionary, a jingoist—if we care to base our charges upon selections of judiciously isolated, highly-colored statements. But, torn from the artistic pattern of which they are integral parts, such statements are no true interpretation of Gierke's opinion.

---

[22] *Das deutsche Genossenschaftsrecht*, I, p. 1.
[23] "Die Grundbegriffe des Staatsrechts . . . ," pp. 154-155.

CHAPTER II

Gierke's dogmatic conclusions are so closely tied up with the historical research out of which they grow that some notion of the latter is absolutely prerequisite to any understanding of the former. I wish, therefore, to summarize here as briefly as possible the more significant findings of the four volumes of *Das deutsche Genossenschaftsrecht*.[1]

"What man is he owes to the association of man with man." This first sentence of *Das deutsche Genossenschaftsrecht* might well be taken as the theme of the whole study. The movement from multiplicity to unity through ever-widening associations may almost be taken as an abbreviation for the movement of history itself. But the principle of unity is but one of the moving forces in the continued development toward association. The other and equally important force is "the idea of liberty."

> But this development from apparently unconquerable variety to *unity* presents only one side of social progress. All spiritual life, all human endeavors would perforce perish if the idea of unity were alone and exclusively triumphant.. With equal force and equal necessity, the

---

[1] Volume I, *Rechtsgeschichte der deutschen Genossenschaft* (1868), is an institutional survey of the development of German associations, carrying the account from the earliest records to the date of publication.

Volume II, *Geschichte des deutschen Körperschaftsbegriff* (1873), discusses the theory implicit in German association law before the Reception. It is "a history of the concept of corporation in its widest sense and the development of this concept into a concept of the state." (p. vii)

Volume III, *Der Staats- und Korporationslehre des Alterthums und des Mittelalters und ihre Aufnahme in Deutschland* (1881), deals only to a very limited extent with German law. At this point in his research, Gierke was forced to make a close study of Roman Law and medieval philosophy in order to trace their influence upon the German theory of corporation.

Volume IV, *Die Staats- und Korporationslehre der Neuzeit* (1913), carries the account of the development of the theory of corporation to the middle of the seventeenth century and then continues the discussion of Natural Law theory to the beginning of the nineteenth century. One section of this volume contains practically a repetition of material published in 1880 under the title *Johannes Althusius und die Entwicklung der naturrechtlichen Staatstheorien*.

A final volume on modern corporation theory and a revision of Volume I, bringing it up to date, were included in Gierke's plans; but other studies prevented completion of his ambitious project. Much of the material which would have been included in Volume V is, however, to be found in Gierke's other works.

opposing idea breaks its way: the idea of persistent multiplicity in every realized unity, of individuality still persisting in the generality, the idea of the rights and independence of all the narrower unities converging in the higher unity, even those of single individuals—the idea of *liberty*.[2]

The conflict of these two principles, unity and liberty, a conflict which, broadly interpreted, includes almost the whole of legal, if not general, history, is the story Gierke attempts to trace. At different levels of complexity the conflict presents itself in a series of shifting antitheses with partial reconciliations: in the antithesis between the unifying authority of the head of the household and the traditional rights and control of larger family units, in similar antitheses between the king and the tribe, between the king and the "nation" of numerous tribes, between feudal lords and a multitude of voluntary associations, between authoritarian institutions of the Church and more spontaneously organized Church orders, between king or emperor and confederations of towns, between modern king and parliament, between modern state and corporation.

Gierke confines his story to Germany because, while he finds in Germany at different periods the highest development of both principles and, therefore, the sharpest antithesis, he also finds in Germany the most hopeful promise of eventual harmony. It is through the Germanic gift of spontaneous organization, the building from below of associations which develop an independent life of their own without crushing out the independent personalities of the individuals or more narrow associations included, that the antithesis is to be solved. If we discount some exaggerations of expression, later corrected by detail, the best and most concise statement of Gierke's point of departure can be given in his own words:

> Of all peoples mentioned in history, none has been so deeply and strongly affected by the antithesis described, none is by its inmost nature so capable of developing both ideas and therefore eventually harmonizing them, as is the Germanic. . . . Inferior to no other people in their bent towards universality and in their capacity for political organization, superior to most in their love of freedom, the Germans above all others have a gift through which they have invested the idea of freedom with a special significance and based the idea of unity on

---

[2] *Das deutsche Genossenschaftsrecht*, I, p. 1.

a solid foundation—this is the gift of organizing associations. . . . That
inexhaustible Germanic spirit of association . . . knows how to secure for
all narrower members of the state an original, independent life, and
yet has the further power to create out of the still uncontrolled elements
of national strength, for the most general as for the most particular
purposes of human existence, an incalculable wealth of associations
which are not animated from above but act spontaneously.

These narrower communities and associations, which in relation to the
universal association (*Allgemeinheit*) appear as particulars, but in relation to their members as universals, offer the only possibility of uniting a large and inclusive state-unity with active civil liberty, with self-
government. Their absence is the chief reason why so many Latin peoples lack civil liberty, their presence the surest safeguard of English and
American liberty. Our German nation has suffered longer and more
deeply under the antithesis than its sister nations, although it has
equally, or perhaps *because* it has developed even more thoroughly than
they those basic Germanic concepts which strive toward universality as
well as individual freedom, uniting both by means of the association.
. . . But the vigorous progress of our own day demonstrates that the
German people recognizes its twofold goal, and permits us to hope that
the latest among the unified European states will be the most perfect.[3]

For the sake of convenience, Gierke arbitrarily divides the
history of the German association into four periods. The main
currents of these periods I wish to summarize here for convenience in later references.

The first period extends to the date of the coronation of Charlemagne. According to Gierke, the basic form of an association
during this period was the free association (*freie Genossenschaft*)
of the old Germanic law—a union resting upon natural coherence
in which all right remains with the collectivity itself.[4] "In the old
Genossenschaft there was no unit distinct from the sum of all the
associates. The abstraction of a state or a separate community
(*Gemeinwesen*) was unknown."[5] "The community of people
(*Volksgenossenschaft*), which took the place of a state for the
Germans, was identical with the sum of all free men who bore
arms. . . . All free men as associates had equal rights and duties,
for each was in like degree the bearer, the guardian, the defender
of the peace and law of the people."[6]

---

[3] Introduction to *Das deutsche Genossenschaftsrecht*, I. pp. 3-4.
[4] *Das deutsche Genossenschaftsrecht*, I, p. 9.
[5] *Ibid.*, I. p. 45.
[6] *Ibid.*, I, p. 35.

The community of people was at no time a unitary whole. Within it were the clan and the mark-community as the most intimate associations, and, between these and the whole, intermediate associations of which the most common was the hundred. Each of these more restricted associations was also a personal union of individuals, in which the individuals formed the united whole; there existed no whole distinct from the individuals.[7]

But from the beginning there existed side by side with the associational union and in opposition to it the opposite form of organization, the lordly union (*herrschaftlicher Verband*). The lordly union Gierke defined as a form of organization in which one individual occupies the position which in the *Genossenschaft* is occupied by all associates. "One individual—and this individual not as the embodiment of an abstract idea, but as a living personality—is the *Master* (*Herr*) and himself represents the complete legal unity of the group. He appears as the *head*; through him and in him the multiplicity is bound together. Law, order, and authority in the union come from him . . . he alone represents the union as such externally and internally. . . ."[8]

Like the associational-union the lordly union goes back to the family in its origin. It is the development and expansion of the patriarchal household principle, while the *Genossenschaft* is the development of the clan principle. In the wider family group the head of the house is merely an associate, but in his own household he is the master. "The German household was, as in all periods and with all peoples, organized as a unit. The head of the household is alone the source, the holder, the guardian of the peace and law prevailing in the union, he is the exclusive representative of the unity of the group. . . . He is the *master*; others are his servants."[9]

During this first period the struggle between Gierke's two general principles takes the form of a struggle between these two types of organization. There is a crossing of the two tendencies, as when a dominant leader gains a position of complete control in a *Genossenschaft* or when a lord's men organize on an associational basis; but there is no amalgamation. The two exist side by

---

[7] *Ibid.*, I, pp. 39 ff.
[8] *Ibid.*, I, p. 89.
[9] *Ibid.*, I, p. 15; *cf.* p. 12, pp. 89-90.

side until the principle of lordship gradually crowds out the principle of association.[10]

The second period, from 800 to 1200, is the period of the definite triumph of the *Herrschaft* over the *Genossenschaft* as the dominant principle of organization. The building up by nobles or families of bands of followers directly dependent upon them, a type of organization which existed early enough for Tacitus' record, becomes the prevailing type. Protection, favors, honor from the lord; service, loyalty from the follower become the driving thoughts of the whole life of the nation. Even religion, poetry, custom, morality are brought within the ideological circle of loyalty and service, and thus to the support of the prevailing legal relationships.[11] "Everything which tends to secure victory in an historical process was on the side of the new thought, and irresistibly it pushed out from the royal palace and noble court into the most remote mark of the nation."[12]

The victory of the *Herrschaft* is demonstrated at the top by the transformation in the idea of kingship. The kingship, Gierke tells us, was originally a *Genossenschaft* institution; the king was a folk-king; the folk-law was the source of his power; he was not the lord, the master, of the association which was the people, but simply the highest judge and leader.[13] But together with his position as leader of an association, excercising power emanating from the association, the king had always possessed a second and quite different capacity as head of the greatest household and court in the land. In the latter capacity he was the lord, his authority over his household and court servants was original and practically absolute. Reenforced by the necessity for strong centralized control, the *Herrschaft* relationship spread from the king's household and gradually replaced the earlier associational relationship between king and people. "From this start it was possible for the king, supported by the Church and the Roman influence, to carry his lordly authority into ever wider circles, until at last he faced his whole people as their lord and they faced him as subjects."[14] The king's household servants became public officials; the king's retainers became the national army and took the place of "the

[10] *Ibid.*, I, p. 13.
[11] *Cf. ibid.*, I, pp. 98, 193.
[12] *Ibid.*, I, p. 100.
[13] *Ibid.*, I, p. 101.
[14] *Ibid.*, I, p. 102.

people in arms."[15] It is the same process in Germany as proceeded with less interruption to an earlier conclusion in England.

From the top down, the same process is repeated all along the line, until finally "the whole people is formed into a great union of lords and subjects in which each lord is at the same time the subject of another lord, that lord indirectly the subject of the lord of his lord and finally of the king . . . a union in which a great ladder leads from below all the way to the throne, finally, indeed, to heaven itself."[16]

Toward the end of the second period had appeared a new principle of organization, different alike from the old associational principle and from the feudal principle of lordship. It is this new principle, the principle of the free union (*der freie Vereinigung* or *der Einung*) which dominates the period between 1200 and 1525.

The old *Genossenschaft* had grown out of the natural coherence of the group associated; the new free union grew out of the free will of the associates. "That an association does not, or at least not entirely, owe its existence to natural coherence, nor to an external unity coming through a lord, but finds the final basis of its solidarity in the free will of the associates, that was the new thought which built from below a many-membered, popular structure during the last three centuries of the Middle Ages while the older structures crumbled steadily to ruin."[17]

The medieval gild is the purest example of this new type of organization. While it differed significantly from the older association in having a free-will instead of a natural basis, it resembled the older association in two ways. In the first place, it had, like the older association, always a general purpose or set of purposes. It was not an organization for realizing one particular goal; it had a wide range of interests and purposes, economic, religious, social, ethical, political.[18] Before its later degeneration, then, the medieval association differed considerably from modern associations, which are invariably organized for some specific purpose.[19] The medieval association resembled the older association also in its organization. The law, rights, duties of the association were attributes of the collective membership. As in the

[15] *Ibid.*, I, pp. 103 ff.
[16] *Ibid.*, I, p. 121.
[17] *Ibid.*, I, p. 221.
[18] *Ibid.*, I, p. 228.
[19] *Cf. ibid.*, I, p. 450.

Gemeinde and the nation, the collective whole appeared only in the assembly of the associates.[20] In the trade gilds, for example, "the real bearer of the collective associational rights, the source of all law and order was the assembly of the full-associates, of the free masters entitled to engage in the craft."[21]

The principle of free union plays a most significant role in directing the development of medieval German towns. With the winning of freedom during the thirteenth and fourteenth centuries came an amalgamation in town constitutions of the impersonal element of territory and the personal element of citizenship. The former was the principle of the old *Markgemeinde* and was, of course, one of the most important feudal principles. The latter was the older Germanic principle. Their fusion through the new idea of the *Einung* finally made the town a territorial and juristic person—the forerunner of the modern political state. Of the concept of corporation developed in and for the towns we shall have more to say later.

Within the unit of the town there was still room for a manifold, independent associational life in the form of merchant and craft gilds.[22] And by the side of gilds based upon the stable foundation of necessary and important trades or crafts, arose gilds and associations of every degree of permanence, importance, and respectability. Gierke finds records not only of the famous *Meistersänger* gild recognized by Charles IV and granted its own coat of arms,[23] but also of gilds of beggars, robbers, and pirates,[24] and of temporary gilds formed for the duration of a dangerous land journey or sea voyage.[25] He finds even the interesting record of seven young men who in 1343 solemnly bound themselves together and swore "not to rest before they had squandered their money in dissipation."[26]

The town itself was often but one member of a larger association. The numerous federally organized city leagues of the thirteenth to fifteenth centuries were but a realization on a higher

[20] *Ibid.*, I, p. 231.
[21] *Ibid.*, I, p. 398.
[22] *Cf. ibid.*, I, pp. 332 ff.
[23] *Ibid.*, I, pp. 452-453.
[24] *Ibid.*, I, p. 446.
[25] *Ibid.*, I, p. 451.
[26] *Ibid.*, I, p. 453, n. 3.

plane of the principle of free union.[27] "The legal idea of the Hansa," Gierke tells us, for example, "which, to be sure, was but one side of a basis which was also political, economic, ethical, was nothing other than the idea of *an association resting upon a free union of all commercial communities of low-German origin and law.*"[28]

The ideal of free union from below penetrated even into the *Reich*, and gave promise at one time of federal reconstruction from below of the loose and tottering structure of the outworn feudal Empire. But complete unity by this route was impossible so long as one large class, the peasants, were left out of the associational movement.[29] Only in Switzerland, where the older associational unity of rural territories had survived the feudal period, and where the league was from the beginning a union of territorial communities rather than a union of classes or states, was national unity through a federal associational structure possible.[30]

In Germany rural territories remained, with few exceptions,[31] dominated by feudal principles carried over from the preceding period. Between the remnants of this feudal *Herrschaft* principle and the vital associational principle of the time there could be no permanent peace. To achieve national unity one or the other had to be exclusively successful. It was a modified *Herrschaft* principle which finally brought some degree of unity in the next period.

During the fifteenth and sixteenth centuries began a transformation in the medieval associational spirit which gradually killed its vitality and broke its resistance to the new authoritarianism which ushered in the modern era of the national state.

"The German associational system of this period long outlasted the Middle Ages in outer form, and has come down in many institutions to our own day. But external continuity scarcely concealed the radical transformation which took place in the content

[27] The total number of city leagues was extremely large, but the three leagues of any importance were the Rhine League, the Swabian League, and the Hansa. *Ibid.*, I, pp. 463-487; *cf.* Georg von Below, *Das ältere deutsche Städtewesen und Burgertum* (1898), pp. 13-14.
[28] *Das deutsche Genossenschaftsrecht*, I, p. 472.
[29] "Indeed a territorial state structure resting on a pure community constitution was impossible in the greater part of Germany, because the whole rural population had no share in the association movement. The great mass of the peasants only sank more deeply into subjection with the separation of town and country." *Ibid.*, I, p. 514; *cf. ibid.*, I, pp. 509, 10.
[30] *Ibid.*, I, p. 532.
[31] *Ibid.*, I, p. 515.

and spirit of the associational movement after the fifteenth and
sixteenth centuries. The system of free associations developed into
a system of privileged corporations."[32] "Ever sharper became the
distinctions between classes which associations had once sought to
unite; ever closer did the association draw the line of membership; ever more prominent became the particularity of its purpose
over its generality. A system of privileged corporations extending
into the whole nation, transforming the living members of a great
national organism into purely individual organisms, threatened
public life with pettiness, disruption, and destruction, until finally
consideration of the commonweal could only be brought to the
front through territorial authority developed into princely absolutism, and through ruthless demolition of associations standing between the state and the individual."[33] With the sense of nationality
almost completely lost, with the idea of the state dissipated in a
multitude of petty principalities, with a system of nobility dominated by pride of caste and lackeyism, with once proud burghers
transformed into petty provincials and a proud commercial spirit
into a petty shop-keeper attitude, with the pride in craftsmanship
pushed aside by a greedy, monopolistic gild spirit—with every
class dominated by short-sighted self-interest to be realized by pur-
chasable privilege—"the people has become a sum of individuals,
even the idea of community has been almost lost to them."[34]

The fourth period, then, is the period of authority (*Obrigkeit*),
developing, with the help of Roman and Canon Law, into state
absolutism. At the beginning of the period ruthless authority from
above is invited not only by the selfish pettiness of petrified associations, but also by the period of lawless violence accompanying
and following the Reformation, the peasants' revolts, and the religious wars. For the maintenance of any degree of order, strong
centralized authority has become necessary.

The distinguishing characteristic of the new authoritarian
principle, an intensification of the older *Herrschaft* principle, was
the concentration of all political power in an abstract "state" which
was something set apart from the people of a nation. Since the
state becomes the exclusive representative of the common interest,
alone endowed with the function of maintaining order and justice,

[32] *Ibid.*, I, pp. 297-298.
[33] *Ibid.*, I, p. 583; *cf.* also pp. 583-637.
[34] *Ibid.*, I, p. 641.

there can exist no rival centers of authority. Possible rivals standing between state and individuals must be abolished or completely
dominated from above by the state.[35]

> Whereas the free community of the German law had recognized the
> associations of its citizens as communities homogeneous with the whole,
> and left them an independent life of their own, even where they be-
> came units in a larger composite structure, the authoritarian principle
> strives with rigid consistency towards two goals. It seeks, in the
> first place, to draw into the state concept all political significance of
> *Gemeinde* and corporations. In the second place, it seeks to resolve
> all that may still remain of original significance in associations into the
> concept of a capacity loaned by the state.[36]

The final absorption or dissolution of privileged corporations
by the modern sovereign state[37] left the way open at the end of
this period for the modern free association based upon the individual liberty of all subjects.[38] Discussion of the modern association in Germany will take us into Gierke's theory of what the
nature of the association really is.

---

[35] *Ibid.*, I, pp. 642-643.
[36] *Ibid.*, I, p. 644.
[37] *Cf. ibid.*, I, pp. 883 ff.; *cf., e.g.*, the French *Code pénal* (Sept., 1791), arts. 291-294,
which forbade associations of more than twenty persons without the approval of the government. *Cf.* Maitland, *Collected Papers.* (1911) III, pp. 312 ff.
[38] *Das deutsche Genossenschaftsrecht*, I, p. 11.

CHAPTER III

HISTORICAL BASIS FOR THE GENOSSENSCHAFT-THEORY: THE
GERMAN ASSOCIATION THEORY

The undefined theory implied in the law of the old German association was extremely simple and realistic. The collective membership, the sum of the associates, was the association and the subject of all common rights or powers of the association. The law recognized no collective entity which could be distinguished from its members.[1]

But Gierke warns us repeatedly that there was no clearly defined concept of the association or corporation in early German law. A theory of the corporation can only be constructed artificially from the implications of custom and usage. To read conscious theory into the early law is to add a legal sophistication which was not really there. For the early Germanic law was folk-law, and, therefore, not abstract, subtle, theoretical, but concrete, direct, and substantial.[2]

The beginning of reflection in German law is to be noticed for the first time, Gierke tells us, during the Hohenstaufen period; that is, toward the end of his second historical period.[3] Here begins the long process through which the association is differentiated from its individual members and the individual eventually freed from the bonds of the collectivity.[4] It is a process which, during the lively period of the later middle ages, proceeded along Germanic lines rather than foreign. Gierke realizes that Germanic

---

[1] "We have found the nature of the old *Genossenschaft* to reside in the fact that the collectivity itself was set up as the subject of law without differentiating its unitary and multiple sides . . . ." *Das deutsche Genossenschaftsrecht*, II, p. 134.
"We have seen how, on one side. the *Genossenschaft* was identified with the collectivity of associates; and, on the other side, the collective law contains within itself the content of the special associational law." *Ibid.*, II, pp. 266-267.
Cf. pp 28-29 *supra*: cf. Gierke. *Deutsches Privatrecht*, I, p. 457.
[2] *Cf. Das deutsche Genossenschaftsrecht*, II, pp. 12-14.
[3] "With the Hohenstaufen period the German folk-consciousness turned in its legal and constitutional life, as in every other field, toward more abstract thought, reflection upon itself, and systematic organization. Here for the first time our people began consciously to model relations after the idea. Where formerly natural forces seemed to hold sway, man, acting upon a basis of rational consideration, now assumes a creative role, begins to advise and decide, to alter and improve." *Ibid.*, II, p. 14.
[4] *Ibid.*, II, p. 14.

ideas were often lent a Roman color through the clothing of Latin terminology. Especially was this true in the Empire and in describing imperial institutions. But, Gierke insists, the jurists, while they wrote Latin, thought German. They used the stereotyped juristic phraseology of the Roman Empire with no realization of the technical implications of the phrases. They spoke, for example, of a *res publica* or *civitas,* but it would have been as difficult for them to understand under the term an abstract, invisible "state" as it would be for us to dissociate this concept from the word. They ascribed property rights to the *fiscus,* but would have been astonished at the suggestion that they thereby ascribed to the state a special personality, that they were setting up a juristic person as a subject of law.[5] In so far as there was a carryover from the dying Roman Empire, it was a formal carrying over of terminology rather than an adoption of ideas. The real "Romanization" of German law came only with the Reception.

During the Hohenstaufen period, then, a period marked by rapid economic and social changes, begins a new epoch in German law and political theory. Simple, concrete principles of folk-law are reworked into abstract concepts; concepts are distilled out of concrete instances; abstract concepts of the state and of law appear on the scene; public and private law are differentiated; legislation and constitutions are deliberately constructed; political offices and civil rights come into prominence; personal freedom and freedom of property become the pivotal points of private law. In short, the many-sided development away from primitive concreteness towards reflection, abstraction, differentiation, formulation—the development usually ascribed solely to the influence of the Reception—begins, says Gierke, in this early period, and proceeds along German lines.[6] The failure to coordinate these developments into a common German law came not from the poverty of German legal principles or the weakness of German reflection upon law; but, as we shall see later, from the unequal development of legal principles in different parts of a nation so minutely divided in territory and so sharply divided into classes.[7]

It is, of course, in the towns that we find the strongest and earliest evidence of this new development. And it is in the towns

_____

[5] *Ibid.,* II, pp. 15-16.
[6] *Ibid.,* II, p. 20.
[7] *Cf. ibid.,* II, pp. 19-20.

that we find the earliest approach toward a theory of the corporation which goes beyond the naive, realistic assumptions of early
German law. It is in the towns that the collective unit itself becomes a personality existing outside its individual members—an
invisible personality possessing legal rights and political power.
For the first time it is recognized that there can exist a subject of
rights and wielder of power which is neither a group of individuals
nor a single lord.[8]

This town personality was based upon territory and the associational personal union of the citizenry. Town personality thus
grew out of factors which had earlier given rise to the *Herrschaft*-
union on the one hand and the *Genossenschaft*-union on the other.[9]
The town was, further, a composite "living organism" made up of
lesser associations and of its own organs of administration. The
unity of the town and the unified personality immanent in the structure of the town was always a composite, organically conceived
unity.[10]

This unified personality was, to be sure, something distinct
from all the factors that went into its making. That is the important step in the development of theory which Gierke stresses here.
"It remained the same town even when its territory, its citizenry,
its organization changed."[11] Such a personality, while it might
be considered an abstraction, had about it nothing of artificiality or
fiction. "In the elevation of the town into a person there was nothing artificial or fictitious. . . . There was, however, an abstraction, since only by means of abstraction could unity be discovered
in multiplicity and set forth as something distinct from it."[12]

But while the town was recognized as a distinct personality, the
abstraction was not yet pushed to the point, reached in Roman law,
where the juristic-personality swallowed up its component elements. It is in the harmonizing of unity with plurality, and in

---

[8] "The town in its invisible *unity* was the subject of political rights; these rights it
held, however, as a *collectivity* standing above individuals . . . . The town as such was
also the subject of political power as against individual citizens and narrower civil associations. And herein it differentiated itself from all previously known holders of legal authority.
For here for the first time it was an invisible unity residing in the collectivity that was
considered as the holder of authority. Here for the first time it was neither a visible
lord nor a physically conceived collectivity nor both in a prescribed relationship which
were the possessors in their own right of political power. But political power adhered to
the town as a town, and only its exercise was delegated by the town constitution to
single town organs." *Ibid.,* II, p. 733.
[9] *Ibid.,* II, pp. 820-821.
[10] *Ibid.,* II, pp. 821-822.
[11] *Ibid.,* II, p. 822.
[12] *Ibid.,* II, p. 823.

the natural acceptance of the proposition that the one can be built out of the many without destroying the identity of the many, that Gierke finds the peculiarly German element of the theory of corporation.

This idea of corporate personality, first brought to more or less conscious formulation in the towns, spread rapidly through all thought on associational life and exerted a strong influence upon the form and legal conception of association within the towns and above the towns. Craft and trade gilds and the *Landesgemeinde* particularly were readily interpreted in terms of this new theory of corporation.

The conception of association or corporation at this point, still purely German, is best summarized in Gierke's own words:

> The essential goal of all corporate organization is the forming of the association into a living *collective personality*. All progress which has been accomplished in the corporate association as distinguished from the old associations leads back to the point that the unity immanent in the association is acknowledged as a person and given legal recognition. . . . The association as such wins a place as a legal entity existing independently of the individual personalities of its members and remaining identical with itself in unchanging continuity even when its members change. The associational entity is a *collective* personality because it is immanent in an associated collectivity from which it arises and without which it could no more exist than could an individual person without a body. But it is no collectivity of persons in the old sense, simply a unity and collectivity at the same time; . . . it is the *unity* in the collectivity conceived as a person. The collective personality is not an artificial entity, but a real entity. . . . [13]

> [The German collective person] was not related to its members as a mere convenient third party, but stood in an organic relation to them. For it existed not merely for its own sake, but also for the sake of its members, and was limited and bound by this fact. On the other hand, the members existed not solely for themselves, but also for the association, and were likewise limited and bound. From this relationship arose the possibility of coordinating the rights of the unit and the rights of its members.[14]

> According to the German legal point of view, it belongs to the nature of the association to exist as unity in plurality, and therefore to lead an independent existence above its members, but at the same time to stand in an organic relation to the plurality of independent entities contained within itself. The association personality as such, therefore,

---

[13] *Ibid.*, II, pp. 886-887; *cf.* also *Deutsches Privatrecht*, I, p. 458.
[14] *Das deutsche Genossenschaftsrecht*, II, p. 40.

stands above, but not outside, the collectivity of individuals which forms for the moment its body. It is a unity contained in them which would evaporate into nothing as an empty abstraction were the relation to the collectivity of independent persons to be thought away. . . .[15]

This progress during the twelfth to fourteenth centuries towards a German conception of corporation never reached the point of clearly defined abstract theory. Like the concepts of early English common law, the concepts of German law still lacked the polished conciseness demanded of the principles of a more highly developed system. And not only was German law at an early stage of development and entirely uncodified; it was also very largely still folk-law with principles modified by divergent local customs. There was no centralized system of kings' courts to help bring the administration of justice in remote regions up to a general standard, to modify local differences, and gradually to weld out of general principles widely accepted an authoritative, if not rigidly codified, common law. Political territorial disunion and class distinctions stood in the way of a development of German law similar to the development of English common law.[16] The native German law "was still rather folk-law than lawyers' law and was dissipating itself in countless local customs."[17]

Such conditions made the reception in Germany of the foreign Roman law not only a possibility, but, according to Gierke, an historical necessity.[18] And the development of a consistent theory of corporation is but a part of the general history of the Reception.

> We shall seek in vain in German law books of the Middle Ages for any independent discussion of the legal nature of collective units (*Gemeinheiten*). What we shall meet of such discussion in medieval Germany decks itself in the paraphernalia of the learned jurisprudence. But the learned jurisprudence does not stand upon the ground of na-

---

[15] *Ibid.*, II, p. 906.
[16] *Cf. ibid.*, II, pp. 14-24
[17] *Cf.* Maitland's contrast of medieval English and medieval German law: Gierke's *Political Theories of the Middle Age*, translated with an introduction by Frederic William Maitland (1927), pp. xii ff.
[18] "German law did not succeed through its own strength in raising itself from confusion and conflict to unity and national scope. This task fell to a foreign law, not because it was a foreign law, but *in spite of* the fact . . . , because it was a *common law*; whereas native law was unable to rise itself into a common law because of the tragic political disunity of Germany. Here and here alone lies the basic cause of the Reception. All other causes advanced explained only the *possibility* of the Reception: its historical *necessity* followed solely from the fact that a common law for the whole nation and all of its classes was unattainable in any other manner." *Das deutsche Genossenschaftsrecht*, II, p. 19.

tional law. Its triumph means for Germany the triumph of a foreign law. The history of the theory of corporations in Germany is therefore a part of the history of the Reception.[19]

While practical burghers were applying legal principles of association, generally accepted but as yet unsystematized, unpolished, and relatively unmeditated, other more ,scholarly groups were at work elaborating in fine detail philosophic theories of human association. Theologians, scholastic philosophers, historians, and, somewhat later, apologists for princely authority drew upon the total body of scholastic thought for principles applicable to political association. The scriptures, St. Augustine and other patristic writings, Aristotle, and, to some extent, the materials of positive jurisprudence served as sources for concepts and arguments which they attempted to reinterpret and reorganize to form a consistent theological-philosophical theory of state and society. In the writings of scholars like St. Thomas, Dante, John of Salisbury, Nicholas of Cusa, and a multitude of others, whom Gierke studied carefully and critically, are to be found many indications of the influence of the Roman civilists and the canonists as well as of Aristotle and Greek thought. But Gierke finds also a substantial residue of political philosophy which may be considered purely medieval. The principles of association upon which the structure of theory was based were, to a large extent, influenced by the principles generally, if inarticulately, recognized, and actually in operation. Yet the scholarly theory of state and society, conceived in terms of the teleological unity which gives order to cosmic multiplicity, was rather far removed from the problems of the burghers and practical lawyers, and the system constructed undoubtedly boasted a degree of perfection not always in conformity with the actual relations existing between emperor and princes, princes and towns, or towns and gilds.

The essential character of this typically "medieval" political thought is thus summarized by Gierke:

> Political thought, when it is *genuinely medieval*, starts from the *whole*, but ascribes an intrinsic value to every *partial whole* down to and including the *individual*. If on the one hand, it touches antique thought when it places the whole before the parts, and on the other hand touches modern theories of natural law when it stresses the intrinsic

---

[19] *Ibid.*, III, pp. 2-3.

and original rights of the individual, its distinctive characteristic is that it sees the universe as an articulated whole and every being—whether a community or an individual—as both a part determined by the universal purpose, and a more restricted whole with a special purpose of its own.[20]

The reconciliation of the special purposes of the partial groups and of individuals with the general purpose of the whole depends, in medieval thought, on the unity of God. He created and governs the multiplicity, and He has assigned to each group and individual a purpose peculiarly its own, yet in harmony with the total purpose of His universe. For an example, Gierke draws on Dante, in whom he finds the typically medieval thought "at its purest and fullest,"[21] and who, he asserts, discusses mankind as a partial group, unified by a common purpose which is not that of the universe as a whole, nor of the single individuals: the "continuous activation of the whole power of reason."[22] This conviction of the unity of mankind as a group within the universe and above the separate individuals Gierke also finds expressed in the frequent references to mankind as a "mystical body" or an "*universitas*."[23] And the medieval conviction of the unity of mankind is only the more emphasized by the conflicts between ecclesiastical and secular authority, as the protagonists of both sides seek to reconcile this apparent duality with the unity they feel to be a necessary concept.

But even as mankind, whether it be regarded as Church or as Empire, is an organic unity within the universe, so within this unity of mankind there exists further multiplicity. The hierarchic structure of the Church provided medieval thinkers with a model for their system of secular organization; and villages, cities, provinces, nations or kingdoms appear as organic groups, each again with its own unity and purpose.

> Between the highest universality and the absolute unity of the individual appear a series of intermediate units, in each of which lesser units are comprised and combined.[24]

Thus the universe is conceived as an hierarchic structure of communities. But the idea of unity dominates the whole, and is reflected in the conception of the subordinate groups.

[20] *Ibid.*, III, p. 514.
[21] *Ibid.*, III, p. 512.
[22] *Ibid.*, III, p. 517, n. 6.
[23] *Ibid.*, III, p. 517.
[24] *Ibid.*, III, p. 545.

5

> To each particular being is assigned its place in the whole, and to each link between beings corresponds a divine decree. But since the world is one organism, animated by one spirit, formed by one ordinance, the same principles that appear in the structure of the world must reappear in the structure of its every part. Therefore every particular being, in so far as it is a whole, appears as a smaller copy of the universal *"macrocosmos"*; it is a *"microcosmos"* or *"mirror mundus."* In the fullest measure this is true of every human individual; but it is true also of every human community and of human society in general.[25]

With the idea of unity dominating the hierarchy, Gierke finds also that the relation of the subordinate group to the whole is conceived as an organic rather than a mechanical articulation.

> Since medieval thought proceeded from the idea of a unitary whole, an *organic conception* of human society was as familiar to it as an atomistic or mechanical construction was originally alien.[26]

This is expressed in the general comparison of mankind to an animate body, a comparison which stresses the harmonious coordination of the particular functions of the partial groups, their interaction, and their cooperative service of the purpose of the whole. But this organic notion of the structure of society does not involve the absorption of the partial groups within the whole, inasmuch as the purpose of the whole does not absorb their particular purposes; thus the structure is one that Gierke describes as federalistic rather than centralized.

> If, however, medieval thought, whenever it was genuinely medieval, postulated the visible unity of mankind in Church and Empire, it regarded this unity as *restricted to those relations in which unity was demanded by the common purpose of mankind*. Therefore this unity was neither absolute nor exclusive, but appeared as the vaulted dome of an organically articulated structure of human society.[27]

Starting with the whole rather than the parts, emphasizing the organic unity of a whole including all mankind and lesser wholes included in that larger, medieval theory was, however, open to the

---

[25] *Ibid.*, III, pp. 514-515.
[26] *Ibid.*, III, p. 546. For further discussion of this point, see pp. 546 ff.; cf. also ibid., III, pp. 108 ff.
[27] *Ibid.*, III, p. 544. It is this section on medieval political theory (vol. III, pp. 502-644) which Maitland translates. Cf. also the concise summary in Gierke, *Johannes Althusius . . .*, pp. 226-227.

centralizing tendencies of classical political theory. Assuming the
unity as a God-given unity in which order is maintained by divine
law, it was given a strong theological tinge which drew it naturally
into close reliance upon centralizing canonist principles. But the
tendency to express the unity of society in terms of monarchy
Gierke regarded as a purely medieval trait deriving in part from
the notion of God as monarch of the universe, but also in harmony
with the old German principle of lordship.[28] This predilection for
monarchy was not incompatible with another Germanic trait of
medieval theory, namely the habit of assuming always "an original
and active right of the group taken as a whole,"[29] and the ascrib-
ing to each group of a necessary and important position as a member of a larger whole.[30] In this, the thought of learned circles came
close to the *Genossenschaft*-theory of practical life.

In short, in order to achieve an all-embracing symmetrical system, the scholars, after basing their structure partly upon the solid
foundation of practice and custom, completed their edifice on the
framework of scholastic metaphysics, and buttressed it with bor-
rowings from classical theory, Roman civilists, and the equally non-
German canonists.

Thus, isolating themselves from the positive law of practice by
their desire for completeness and perfection, they would have been
unable to support the positive common law against the influence
of the Romanist systematizers, even if the added obstacles of political and class differences had not existed. And, having grate-
fully adopted some of the convenient Romanist principles, they
also opened the way for the later deluge of civilist, canonist, and,
finally, natural law principles which remade entirely the medieval
structure of political thought.

Examination and discussion of the Roman theory of corporation, which during the period of the Reception finally pushed
entirely aside German principles of corporation, forms a substantial portion of two volumes of Gierke's history. He discusses
with careful discrimination the development of the civil law in the
hands of medieval glossators, canonists, and "legists," pointing
out that the acceptance of a Roman theory of corporation was

[28] *Cf. Das deutsche Genossenschaftsrecht*, III, pp. 557-568.
[29] *Ibid.*, III, p. 568.
[30] *Ibid.*, III, pp. 553 ff.

facilitated not only by the earlier infiltration of Roman principles into German medieval law which has been noted above, but also by the infiltration of Germanic principles into the Roman law as reworked by Italian commentators. The law received was, however, still Roman law, and law foreign in spirit to the German conception of associations.[31] It is essential then to point out here the salient principles of the Roman law of association and the points at which they contrast with the Germanic conceptions.

As a first important contrast with Germanic law, Gierke notes the early differentiation in Roman jurisprudence between public law and private law. "The distinction between *jus publicum* and *jus privatum,* a distinction never discovered by the Greeks and discovered by the Germans only at the close of a complicated development, stands at the very threshold of Roman legal history."[32] The first was the *jus populi,* the law of the Roman people, the law of the state. *Jus privatum,* built upon the position of the *paterfamilias,* was the law of individuals.

Roman public law, like Greek political philosophy, tended to exalt the state to the point where the individuals who were its members became irrelevant. While men possessed a sphere of freedom in their relations with other men, as citizens they were absorbed into the state. In public law, strictly conceived, there was but one subject—the Roman state. But the state itself was not conceived as a person. During the period of the Republic the state was invariably identified with the Roman people, and later, although the fiction that all authority emanated from the Roman people still persisted, the state was often identified with the person of the Emperor.[33] Since the single and absolute subject of

---

[31] "The Romanist-canonist theory of association found its way into Germany with the learned jurisprudence. And it entered in that form which it had received during the last centuries of the Middle Ages under the hands of Italian jurists.

"Here, as elsewhere, the Reception was made possible because it was not simple Roman law which found acceptance, but the Italian doctrines worked out by long labor to fit the demands of the times. The Italian doctrines, however, . . . were influenced by medieval Germanic elements. And so they could slowly penetrate and come into prominence at a period when, in view of German conditions, the acceptance of pure Roman law would have been simply unthinkable.

"But, in spite of their medieval Germanic elements, these doctrines formed a system of thought *alien in form and content to the German spirit.* For their theoretical bases and their formulated rules grew out of Roman legal sources, and Roman ideas threaded their way through them again and again in their every modification." *Ibid.,* III, pp. 645-646.

[32] *Ibid.,* III, p. 35.

[33] "The *jus publicum* of the Romans recognized in a strict sense but one subject of law: the Roman *state.* The Roman state appears, to be sure, as a *collective unit* enclosing and limiting all personality, but is still never designated or thought of as a *person.*" *Ibid.,* III, p. 43.

"The folk-community remained identical with the state as the subject of law. The idea that the state in its totality was a living organism for whose subjective unity the

public law was the state, and since the state was in no way regarded as a composite or organic structure, a corporate group recognized in public law could possess neither partial independence nor legal personality. "And so every Roman corporation was above all a *public-law* entity, and as such, in accordance with the Roman concept of *jus publicum*, it could derive its particular existence only from the one original and sovereign subject of all public law, and consequently could appear only as a division of the state separated out for a specific purpose. In accordance with its public-law nature, every corporation was a part of the state-whole, and as such appeared to have been formed by the whole and for the whole in conformity with its model."[34]

Nor was there any place to be found with the Roman private law for a concept approaching that of the German *Genossenschaft*. Based upon the rights and obligations of the *paterfamilias*, the private law was individualistic and atomistic. It was through and through a *"jus quod ad singulorum utilitatem spectat"* and took no cognizance of "organic entities." For the private law, "individual persons stand in full isolation as the subjects of separated spheres of right."[35] "Only a man could be a real person, because only he was an individual, and only the individual was a person."[36] The will of the individual subject of private law is as absolute in its own sphere as is the will of the state in its sphere. And the personality of the individual is as unified and indivisible as that of the state in public law.[37] There is little room here for the rights and duties of corporate groups. The private-law rights and duties of associated groups must be reduced always to the rights and duties of the individuals associated. If the private-law relationships of a group of individuals associated in action happen to coincide, that is a coincidence which private-law theory need not explain.[38]

---

assembly of citizens formed but the highest organ did not enter into Roman law." *Ibid.*, III, p. 48.

"... The Romans could not bring themselves to either the term or the concept of *state personality*. They cling to the idea of the *people* and later the Emperor as the subject of law." *Ibid.*, III, p. 50.

[34] *Ibid.*, III, p. 69. "It is a characteristic contrast that to the Romans every *Gemeinde* and corporation constitution appeared to be an image of the state constitution, while to the Germans the state appeared to be an expansion and consolidation of elements appearing in associational and lordly unions." *Ibid.*, III, p. 69, n. 125.

[35] *Ibid.*, III, p. 38.

[36] *Ibid.*, III, p. 103.

[37] *Ibid.*, III, pp. 36 ff.: II, p. 33.

[38] "With this sort of basic concept of legal subjectivity, the Roman private law simply could not develop a *legal concept of associations*. It had to reduce every private-law collectivity to the right or duty of a *number* of subjects, always considering the subjects, however, as *isolated* individuals who were related externally by an identity of right or circumstances but in no way formed a subjective whole." *Ibid.*, III, p. 39.

The association was, then, denied an independent and real personality or "subjectivity" in both public and private law. The absolutistic nature of public law and the atomistic, individualistic nature of private law were equally effective in logically excluding the association. A collectivity of persons could be recognized only as a *societas* or an *universitas*. The *societas* was considered to be a group of persons obligatorily bound together but still retaining their complete independence and legal isolation from each other. The *societas* had no real existence outside the existence of those who composed it. The *universitas* might be considered a real unity in public law, but it could not be considered a real *person* nor could it share in or detract from the personality and independence of its members.[39] In handling the *universitas*, therefore, the private law was forced to construe it as a *fictitious person*.

> Under such circumstances, there existed for the Romans no possibility whatever of attributing a *real* existence to the juristic person. As a public-law creature, the *universitas* was a real unity, but no person. As a private-law subject it was a person, but no real unity. Only a man could be a real person, because only he was an individual, and only the individual was a person. If an *universitas*, although not an individual in its real substance, was set forth as a person and so as an individual, then a non-existent fact was given legal consideration as though it did exist. Thus Roman jurisprudence was finally and inevitably forced to the conclusion that the personality of the *universitas* was a *fiction*. To be sure, the Romans did not reach this point in one step nor formulate the idea in sharp clarity. . . . But the whole structure of their theory of corporation culminated in the principle that here a non-person was personified by positive law. . . . So finally they took the last step which seemed to be necessitated alike by practical necessity and the logic of law. Since the private law required a person as a subject, and since a real person was not to be found, they created by fiction an artificial person existent only in the idea. For a situation in which the whole structure of their private law required a natural individual, yet in which they did not have a natural individual, they introduced an individual created by law into the world of concepts.[40]

The absolute state of Roman public law and the absolute individual of Roman private law, the "concession" origin of corpor-

---

"Roman law knew nothing of the collective rights or collective responsibilities of German law. By the very nature of its concept of persons it was forced to place all unity of subjects in the objective field of control of the sovereign individual." *Ibid.*, III, pp. 40-41.
[39] *Ibid.*, II, pp. 332-333.
[40] *Ibid.*, III, pp. 103-104.

ations, the fictitious personality of corporations—ideas which were logical and necessary conclusions of the legal principles accepted during the Reception—were also ideas well suited to hasten the victory of the authoritarian principle of Gierke's fourth period and completely to bury older Germanic concepts of association.

Gierke finds a second important external influence upon the German theory of association in the Church and the canon law. "The first far-reaching shock befell this [medieval] federalistic structure from the side of Church thought, since this elevated the papal system to the point of complete absorption of the state by the Church on the one side, and on the other, to a centralization within the Church which was deadening to the independent life of its members."[41]

In Church organization and theory Gierke finds certain elements analogous to the Germanic organic concept of association. The theological-juristic concept of the Church as the body of Christ—"a body with many members, each of which in its own place serves the whole in a special manner, and the least of which is of value to the whole"—was a conception whose influence is obvious in the medieval writers who built the "federalistic structure" of thought later attacked by Church and state.[42] Within the Church Gierke finds occasional evidence of orders organized from below upon a model similar to that of the earlier gilds.[43] And during the Conciliar Movement he finds an attempt on the part of the more radical theorists, following the path which in worldly politics led to a brand of popular sovereignty, to realize in practice what we might term the associational implications of the doctrine that the Church was "the Congregation of the Faithful." To Gerson, Zabarella, and others, the Council represented the Universal Church, and its constitutional power was conceived as more basic and original, and, therefore, superior to that of the pope. And Nicholas of Cusa, extending to Church organization his natural-law principles of election and consent as the bases of authority, finds the Council representing (or standing in the place of) the Universal Church, since the members of the Council represent their respective communities which together comprise the Universal Church.[44] There is here certainly a strong suggestion of that

---

[41] *Johannes Althusius* . . . , pp. 227-228.
[42] *Cf. Das Wesen der menschlichen Verbände*, p. 14.
[43] *Cf. Das deutsche Genossenschaftsrecht*, I, pp. 285 ff.
[44] *Ibid.*, III, pp. 581-595; *cf.* Maitland, *op. cit.*, pp. 49-61.

type of federalistic structure which Althusius developed later, but Gierke does not expand the point here.

The spirit which dominated Church organization and permeated Church theory and law, however, was the spirit of the classical and authoritarian state, rather than the spirit of the medieval *Genossenschaft*. The Church, the Christian Community, was monarchic, with God its King and God's will its law. Member churches and church orders stood in the same relation to the Universal Church as did Roman corporations to the state. "Every right and all power was effective as loaned from above, and was exercised by every subordinate in the name of a superior and finally in the name of God. He who belonged to the Church belonged to the great Kingdom of God. . . . God Himself was the heavenly King and His son and heir the co-ruler of this kingdom."[45]

> When, in accordance with its broad basis, the Church is identified with the Congregation of Believers and is defined even by the canonists as *"congregatio fidelium,"* still, in the heyday of the canon law particularly, it was maintained that all the life and unity of the Church first came into existence with the institution established from above and outside the generality. The Church appears as a divine institution; and its whole structure and organization rests not upon an associational basis, but upon a directly divine investiture. . . . The Church is the mystical body, whose head is Christ; it is the all-inclusive kingdom of God, ruled by the divine king. It would crumble away lifeless were its union with its transcendental center of will severed.[46]

> It is well known that the institutional idea prevailed over the associational idea in the concept of the *universal Church.* When the Church was represented as the Congregation of Believers and so as *coetus universalis,* or *universitas,* what was referred to was merely its passive sphere of operation, only the basis of the mystical body. Its living unity lay in its divine head and the earthly representatives of this head. The basis of its unity . . . is not the unified will of its members, but the one will of its founder.[47]

Such conceptions, developed to explain relations within the Church, the canonists translated into the field of worldly relations. Worldly associations of men they construed as members of one great collective body which itself owed its existence to divine institution.[48] "Thus the canonists implanted in the theory of corpora-

---

[45] *Ibid.,* I, p. 144.
[46] *Ibid.,* III, pp. 248-249.
[47] *Ibid.,* II, p. 555.
[48] *Cf. ibid.,* III, p. 276.

tion the idea that corporation rights and above all the legal subjectivity of an association were consequences of an *authoritarian
donation*. It is a *'concessio superioris,'* ordinarily a special concession for the single association, but possibly also a general legislative concession, which establishes the *universitas* as such, which
makes it a juristic person."[49] Thus the conclusions of the canonists in regard to earthly associations readily corresponded with
those of the Romanists, and a theory of corporation built upon the
two systems remained dominant for several centuries and has not
been without extensive influence in modern times.[50]

While Roman and canonist principles, entering German law
with full force during the late fifteenth and sixteenth centuries
when doctrines of princely absolutism needed theoretical support,
were stripping from associations every vestige of original and independent authority, an opposite school of thought, developing
doctrines of natural law and the social contract, was equally effective in attacking from below all associations which intruded between the individual and the state.

Natural-law doctrines, which became increasingly important
after the middle of the seventeenth century, led to two distinct lines
of development as related to the position of associations. On the
one hand, the state, like all other human associations, might be
constructed according to the same principle, the principle of social
contract; and on the basis of free contract a writer like Althusius
might reproduce something very similar to the medieval federalistic conception of society.[51]

But the more important development of the contract theory
was one which appealed directly to the individual as the basis of
state authority, without the interposition of intermediary associations—which, in fact, finally attacked intermediary associations
as supporters of royal absolutism. The appeal to the naked indi-

---

[49] *Ibid.*, III, p. 290.

[50] "Th Romanist-canonist theory of corporation developed in the Middle Ages . . . remained the ruling doctrine in European jurisprudence until after the middle of the seventeenth century." *Ibid.*, IV, p. 1.

[51] "He developed fully the idea of contract for corporation, *Gemeinde*, and state, all
of which he pictured as free-will associations, although they were conditioned by man's
social nature. . . . And thus he portrayed in full relief the ultimate philosophic consequences
of the contract idea, and deduced all right of the community from the innate right of human
individuals. Even the sovereign rights of the state are for him finally but the product of
individual right freely surrendered and made common. A qualification of this individualistic
basic principle was made possible only by the assumption that the state received its war-
rant of power not directly but through a series of indispensable intermediary groups of
individuals." *Johannes Althusius . . .*, pp. 99-100. *Cf.* discussion of Althusius in Ch.
VII, *infra*.

vidual, which, Gierke tells us, distinguished the theory of Hobbes,[52] led the contract writers with few exceptions to an extreme
individualism which made anything but a "mechanical" conception
of corporations impossible.

> Ever more decisively it appeared as an unavoidable basic element of
> the social contract theory that theoretically *the community must be
> derived from the individual*. If one wished to remain true to himself,
> he was obliged to cling to the principles that the individual man was
> older than the association, that every association was the product of a
> sum of individual acts, and that all corporate rights, including even the
> authority of the state, were abstracts of differentiated and combined in-
> dividual rights.[53]
>
> The doctrine of social contract was obliged to define this individual-
> istic foundation of the state more closely in that the legal basis of all
> political union was laid in the *free will* of the individual. For it pro-
> ceeded from the assumption of a pre-political state of nature, in the de-
> scription of which it lost itself in endless controversy, but always agreed
> in the acceptance of an original *freedom* and *equality* of men and the
> resulting original *sovereignty* of the individual.[54]

Hence, while natural-law writers were able to tear down the
structure of corporation theory erected by Romanists and canonists
and to destroy finally the notion of fictitious personality, they had
nothing to put in the place of the Romanist concept but a rather
vague concept of the "moral person." Given the completely individualist basis of the school, it was impossible to attribute a real
personality to such a moral person; the personality of the association had to remain with the associated members, as had been the
case in early Roman private law. The association remained a mechanical union of theoretically isolated individuals.[55]

The most significant practical results of the theory are, of
course, to be found in France. Gierke points out that Turgot in
1757 maintained that the moral person, in contrast to the individual, had no rights whatever as against the state.[56] Rousseau
labelled all subordinate or partial organizations as falsifications of
the general will, and set up as a goal the abolition of all corpora-

[52] *Johannes Althusius* . . . , p. 252.
[53] *Ibid.*, p. 105.
[54] *Ibid.*, p. 107.
[55] *Cf. Das deutsche Genossenschaftsrecht*, IV, pp. 443-444.
[56] *Encyclopédie*, VII, p. 75, sec. 6; cited by Gierke in *Das deutsche Genossenschafts-recht*, IV, p. 494.

tions within the state.[57] And the theory was translated into practice in the well-known legislation of 1791.

In Germany the tendency which culminated in the Revolutionary Association Laws in France was supported by absolutistic doctrines from above and natural rights doctrines from below.

> Here also every security of traditional rights tended to disappear be-
> fore natural rights, which alone were regarded as eternal and sacred;
> more and more there appeared as natural rights merely human rights on
> the one hand and the sovereignty of the civil community on the other;
> more and more these great struggling principles were fused together
> in the war of extermination against the independent intermediary mem-
> bers, in which the state discerned an unbearable limitation upon its
> sovereignty and the individual an annoying chain upon his freedom
> and equality. Under the influence of the French Revolutionary doctrine,
> even *Fichte* was unable to rise to a higher vision at precisely this point;
> nor did *Kant* know how to restore through a new, living principle of
> social unification the corporation which he had identified with the foun-
> dation and radically destroyed.[58]

To be sure, Gierke finds among the German jurists of the
eighteenth century some who seemed to follow the lead of Althusius in attempting to build from below, and upon a contract basis,
an associational structure wherein communities more restricted
than the state existed of their own right and with their own spheres
of original rights. Among such jurists he mentions particularly
J. H. Boehmer, Wolff, and especially Nettelbladt who "postulated
a natural-law sphere of existence for the narrower association as
well as for the individual and the state and hence ascribed to it original social rights," and who was, therefore, "in a position to draw
up a system of social organization on the basis of free association which in many respects reproduced the ideas of Althusius."[59]
To this group Gierke adds also Justus Möser, Schlözer, and even
Wilhelm von Humboldt.

But with Savigny and the new school of critical Romanists
came the fresh attempt to "purify" German law of inconsistent
compromises and to bring it back to the strict principles of the
civil law. And this new Romanism, coming at the beginning of
the nineteenth century, entered the scene at exactly the period

---

[57] *Cf. Contrat Social*, Book II, Ch. 3; Book IV, Ch. I; *cf.* Gierke, *Das deutsche
Genossenschaftsrecht*, IV, p. 495.
[58] *Johannes Althusius . . . ,* pp. 257-258.
[59] *Cf. ibid.*, p. 260.

when the German *Genossenschaft* was being reborn, in fact if not in theory. With the dissolution of older privileged corporations, came also the destruction of privileges and inequalities before the law, and the establishment of civil liberty and legal equality—conditions inviting the rise of "the free association in its modern form." It is for the new and rich associational movement of the modern German state that Gierke wishes to elaborate a modern German theory which shall free it from the restrictions implicit in the approach of the Romanists, and which shall utilize German principles and traditions in moving toward the eventual goal where a more perfect reconciliation of authority and liberty shall be realized. In the potentiality of the modern German associational spirit he seems to have an enthusiastic faith.

> Little as we have seen of this period [1806-   ], we may say already that its characteristic creative principle is and will be *free association* in its modern form. Through this principle, the German *Genossenschaft* has awakened, after a long death-like slumber, to more vigorous life, and has come to perfection. No longer bound by any class restriction, no longer limited by any exclusiveness, unendingly malleable in form, equally adapted for the noblest and the most trifling, the most far-reaching and the narrowest purpose, enriched by many qualities of Roman law, but contemptuous of the narrow Roman moulds into which theory and practice are ever trying to force it,—it is the reborn ancient association-idea of German law which has brought forth an incalculable complex of new forms of organization and filled the old with a new content. It has had a share in the transforming of the German *Gemeinde* and the German state, which have accomplished their progress so far and will progress further only through a return to the associational basis and through a revival of their associational elements. It is the sole creator of a free form of association which comprehends and refashions every phase of public and private life, which, great as its influence has been in the past, will be greater still in the near and distant future.[60]

[60] *Das deutsche Genossenschaftsrecht*, I, pp. 10-11.

CHAPTER IV

GIERKE'S GENOSSENSCHAFT-THEORY

Upon this carefully laid historical foundation Gierke attempted to construct a theory of association which would cónform with deeply rooted German legal traditions and at the same time meet 'the demands of a modern society. The way had been pointed out by older Germanists, particularly by Gierke's master Beseler, who attacked the fiction theory of corporation and insisted upon a more realistic legal construction.[1]

The premises of the modern civil-law jurists Gierke found philosophically and historically untenable. These premises he summarized briefly as follows:

> Since *Savigny* it has become customary to approach the theory of persons somewhat in this manner. Originally and from a naturalistic point of view, the concept of legal subjectivity coincides with the concept of human individuals. Every human individual has legal capac-ity, and only the human individual.

It is only through positive law that this concept can be modified; and the modification may take the form of completely or partially denying legal subjectivity to some men, on the one hand, or, on the other, of endowing with legal subjectivity something other than single individuals—thus artificially constructing a "juristic person."[2] These principles, says Gierke, may be regarded as philosophic or historical principles. They are equally invalid as either.

> As a *philosophic* basic principle of present law the claim of every man to personality is firmly established. But the second half of this dogma, that the single individual *only* is of himself a person, is ungrounded in legal philosophy, since, as will appear later, the personality of human collective groups is accepted in legal thought.

---

[1] Gierke points out Beseler's development of a modern *Genossenschaft*-theory in the following works of Beseler: *Die Lehre von den Erbvertragen*, I (1835), pp. 76 ff.; *Volksrecht und Juristenrecht* (1843), pp. 158 ff.; *System des gemeinen deutschen Privatrechts* (1847), I, sec. 66 ff.
[2] *Das deutsche Genossenschaftsrecht*, II, p. 25. 'For direct statements of the Romanist doctrines in German law of Savigny, *System* (1840), II pp. 125 ff.; Kierulff. *Theorie des germanisches Civilrechts* (1839), pp. 129 ff.; *Weiske's Rechtslexikon*, II, pp. 65 ff.

But . . . in so far as these doctrines are intended to express an *historic* truth, they are false and fully unusable in every way as points of departure for historical research. "Originally" and "from a naturalistic point of view" there are simply no "persons." Word and concept are lacking until there is accomplished the abstraction, by no means simple, which overlooks the individual and physical differences of many subjective legal entities for the sake of a unified concept. At first there exists only the historical fact that certain centers of will have rights.

If we ask now *who* originally had rights, it appears immediately that the history of all peoples begins with a *folk-law*, none with a law of human individuals. For this reason it is not the individual as a human being but the individual as a member of the folk who first appears as the bearer of rights, and the folk-law is not *a* law, but *the* law.[3]

Not only did Gierke find the premises of the Romanists untenable, he also found their conclusions totally inadequate to explain the role played in modern life by a manifold variety of associations. Starting with their absolute human individual, private-law followers of Savigny might clear their field of all rival collective personalities, and then, as a matter of convenience, create out of thin air fictitious "juristic" personalities for collective groups which insisted upon acquiring collective rights and duties. These conceptual creatures, leading a shadowy existence beside real persons, themselves as incapable of will or action as the child or incurable lunatic, might be allowed to assume in law an attribute which they lacked in reality. And certain public-law realists, disgusted with the "bloodless apparitions" of private law, might attack the personality of the state itself.[4] But does any of this reasoning dispose of corporate persons, Gierke asks. To deny the personality of the state, for example, is to return to a primitive "realism" which can only identify the state with its ruler or rulers —a conclusion which can satisfy only children, primitive peoples, and "cultured old ladies." Nor can the very real existence of the joint-stock companies, the trade unions, or the religious societies be denied.

And so corporate persons will not yield. We should have to endure them if they were phantoms. But is it not possible that their tough resistance demonstrates that they are by no means ghostly shadows, but living creatures? That law, when it treats organized associations as persons, is not disregarding reality, but giving reality more adequate

---

[3] *Das deutsche Genossenschaftsrecht*, II, pp. 25-26.
[4] *Cf. Das Wesen der menschlichen Verbände* (1902), pp. 4-6.

expression? Is it not possible that human associations are real unities which receive through legal recognition of their personality only what corresponds to their real nature?[5]

Gierke's first basic contention is, then, the concept of the corporation as "a real collective person, itself directly capable of willing and acting."[6]

Insistence upon the real personality of the association necessarily involved also a denial of the "concession" theory. The association, like the individual, exists whether the state recognizes it or not. Like that of the individual, its legal subjectivity requires recognition by state law, but the underlying personality of the association is no more created by state or law than is the personality of the individual. The role of the state and of state law is merely declarative, not creative.

> While the law has the power to certify the quality of legal subjectivity, still it is simply not in a position *to create the factual basis of this quality.* . . . It must . . . sift the beings which it will stamp as persons out of those it finds in existence. In this it is bound by no external restrictions. But if it is to remain true to its idea, it can neither attribute personality to creatures of its own choice nor deny it arbitrarily. . . . The law receives the real bearers of will which it clothes with personality *from without.* It can not wake (*stampfen*) either natural or social organisms out of the ground.[7]

Such a collective person may, of course, possess rights and obligations just as an individual person may possess them. And its rights may be defined and safeguarded against encroachments even by the state. An appeal against the authority of the state need not mean, then, as it has always meant in individualistic theory, an appeal to the rights of individuals, but may mean also an appeal to corporate rights.

> Here we find the roots of the principle of basic individual and corporate rights of liberty which not only guarantees to the individual and to associations a certain sphere not to be disturbed by the state, but also

---

[5] *Ibid.*, pp. 9-10.
[6] *Cf. Die Genossenschaftstheorie und die deutsche Rechtssprechung* (1887), pp. 4-5; *cf.* also *ibid.*, pp. 503-607. *Cf.* Maitland, *Collected Papers* (1911), III; pp. 271-404; especially "The Unincorporate Body," pp. 271 ff.; "Moral Personality and Legal Personality," pp. 304 ff.; and "Trust and Corporation," pp. 321 ff.
[7] *Die Genossenschaftstheorie.* . . , pp. 22-23; *cf. ibid.*, pp. 18, 609.

guarantees a sphere of rights which are simply not to be touched by the state.[8]

Gierke's second basic contention is the organic nature of associations whose independent origin and reality he has established to his own satisfaction. The organic theory of human association is, of course, no new discovery of Gierke. He himself traces the development of various types of organic theory in classical political theory, medieval social theory, and modern German theory,[9] and tends to classify all social theory under the two broad categories of "individualistic" and "organic." While deprecating exaggerated statements of the organic theory made by such writers as Bluntschli, still Gierke finds in the organic theory as developed in Germany during the nineteenth century "the greatest achievement of the modern German science of jurisprudence" and "the basis of modern political theory and jurisprudence."

The organic theory, says Gierke, regards the state and other associations as social organisms, whose members are human individuals, standing above single organisms.[10] Such organisms may legitimately be compared with physico-psychical single organisms. But

> rightly understood, nothing more is claimed by the comparison than that we recognize in the social body the unity of life of a whole arising out of separate parts,—such a unity as we do not find elsewhere except in natural living creatures. We do not forget that the inner structure of a whole whose parts are men must be of such a quality that natural structures can not serve as its model; we do not forget that there takes place here a spiritual unification which is established, given form, put into operation, and dissolved by psychically motivated action. . . . But we view the social whole, like the individual organism, as a living structure, and classify the collective community together with the individual creature under the general concept of living creatures.[11]

Gierke realizes that, by straining for clarity, the analogy may occasionally be exaggerated. But the basis of the analogy—the contention that the association has an organic structure, forming

---

[8] "Die Grundbegriffe des Staatsrechts . . . ," p. 324.
[9] Cf., e.g., ibid., pp. 160-164; Das Wesen der menschlichen Verbände, pp. 9 ff.; Das deutsche Genossenschaftsrecht, III, passim. Cf. also E. Kaufmann, Über den Begriff des Organismus in der Staatslehre des 19 Jahrhunderts (1908).
[10] Das Wesen der menschlichen Verbände, p. 12.
[11] Ibid., pp. 15-16.

an acting, willing, *living* unity, he insists is scientifically valid. To the objection that our sensual perception makes us aware of individual men, but tells us nothing of living associations of men, Gierke makes the reply that might well be instinctive for the good German citizen: "We see a regiment marching to ringing music; we notice voters who cast their votes into the urn; at a public demonstration we are roughly pushed back by a squad of policemen;—and we know immediately by these and a hundred other sensual impressions that things are happening which have to do with the continuation of the life of the state."[12] The living unity of the association we can not see nor perceive sensually. But neither can we perceive sensually the whole personality of an individual. Both we apprehend only indirectly through their actions. "Is the real that which is perceptible to the senses? He who maintains this has not crossed the threshold of philosophic reflection!"[13]

To the objection that, since the ultimate nature of the physical organism is still an unsolved mystery, the organic theory adds more of mystery to what it seeks to explain, Gierke replies, "That which we recognize as real must find a place in our rational world, even though its real nature is unexplained and perhaps impossible of explanation. The puzzle of the organism is identical with the puzzle of life. We do not know what life really is. But we can not for that reason exclude the concept of life from science. For we know that life exists."[14]

To be sure, the social organism can act only through its individual members. But it is a basic distinction of the *Genossenschaft*-theory that the members act as *organs* of the whole, not as mere representatives. The organism has no need of external representatives; it wills, speaks, acts through its member-organs, whose position, functions, and powers are matters determined by the laws or rules of the association.

> Legal principles extend to the formation of the organ by the single person or group of persons designated for the time being to act as the organ, to the acquisition and loss of this position, and to the relation of the organic personality to the individual personality of the participants. The legal concept of the organ is of a specific type and not to

---

[12] *Ibid.*, p. 17.
[13] *Ibid.*, p. 18.
[14] *Ibid.*, p. 19.

be confused with the individualistic concept of the representative. Here it is not a matter of a self-sufficient person being represented by another self-sufficient person. But, just as when the eye sees, or the mouth speaks, or the hand grasps, the man sees and speaks and grasps, so, when the organ functions within its proper competence, the living unity of the whole acts directly. Through the organ, then, the invisible collective person appears as a perceptive, deliberating, willing, and acting unit.[15]

There is, however, one basic difference between individual and collective organisms. Law can control individuals only externally, but law can control collective entities internally as well as externally. It can not only control the activity of the organism, but it can also control its structure. It can establish rights and duties involved in membership; it can designate those members authorized to represent legally the whole; it can establish relations between lower and higher collective organisms, and stamp as legal relations between the whole and its constituent parts. On the basis of such a distinction, Gierke speaks of what he calls "social law"—the law that regulates the inner life of associations—in contrast to what he calls "individual law." This is not to be confused with the usual distinction between public law and private law. Public law is but one type of social law. The social law of the state. is reproduced in graduated degrees of authority down to the most restricted authority of the private club.[16] "Every single social institution sets up within its own circle a special law corresponding to its concrete individuality."[17]

The *Genossenschaft* of Gierke's theory may be defined, then, as a unified organism, whose members are individuals or other associations, possessing its own personality, and having an original purpose, will, and sphere of social law.[18] The association, so defined, is obviously as different from the authoritarian union (*herrschaftlicher Verband*),[19] the "privileged corporation,"[20] or

---

[15] *Ibid.*, pp. 28-29; *cf.* also "Die Grundbegriffe des Staatsrechts . . . ," pp. 329-330.
[16] *Das Wesen der menschlichen Verbände*, pp. 26-30; *cf.* fuller treatment in Chapter VI, *infra*.
[17] *Ibid.*, p. 32. I find an interesting parallel between Gierke's treatment of this point and John R. Commons' treatment of the "going concern" with its "working rules." Although starting from a more specialized problem, Prof. Commons' reasoning is closely analogous at numerous points to that of Gierke. *Cf.* Commons, *Legal Foundations of Capitalism*, Ch. V.
[18] For various definitions by Gierke, see *Das deutsche Genossenschaftsrecht*, I, p. 1030; *ibid.*, II, p. 867; "Grundzüge des deutschen Privatrechts," in Holtzendorff's *Encyclopädie der Rechtswissenschaft* (1904), I, p. 446.
[19] *Cf.* p. 29, *supra*.
[20] *Cf.* pp. 33-35, *supra*.

the modern institution (*Anstalt*)[21] as it is from the Romanistic *persona ficta*. And it does not differ essentially from the medieval *Genossenschaft,* except in the usual specialization of its purpose.

In such a conception of the association Gierke finds the key ·to the sort of social organization which alone he finds ethically satisfactory, since it opens the way to the ultimate resolution of the primitive human strivings after unity and liberty. Again and again he emphasizes his stand between the extreme individualist who would dissolve all human relations into mechanical agreements between sovereign persons and the extreme adherents of the organic theory who would ultimately absorb the individual into the social organism—that he might more easily enjoy his freedom. The perfectly egocentric, isolated individual is as much a fiction ·as the *persona ficta*. A man is born "as a member of a family, a race, a community, in short, as a member of a whole." His relations with collective groups increase as he develops, and it is only through association that he can realize his complete development.

> We proceed from the firmly established historical fact that man everywhere and at all times bears within himself the double character of existing as an individual in himself and as a member of a collective association. Neither of these characteristics without the other would have made human beings human beings. Neither the particularity (*Besonderheit*) of the individual nor his membership in the generality can be thought away without denying the nature of man. . . . Man can have no self-consciousness without *at the same time* recognizing himself as a particular and as a part of a generality. . . . And in so far as we attribute purpose to existence, individual human life is neither mere self-purpose nor a mere means for the demands of the association; but we believe that the individual and the generality exist for themselves and at the same time for each other, and that the task of mankind lies in the establishing of harmony between the mutually complementary factors of the particular and the generality.
>
> From this point of view we must attribute to the human individual as well as to the human association full *reality* and a *unitary character*. For us, the individual existing for himself alone and drawing upon himself is a natural and real life-unit. But we find just as natural and

---

[21] Gierke distinguishes between *genossenschaftlich* and *anstaltlich* organization as follows: "The former appears when a group of wills develop a single, unified will from themselves: here the single wills mould themselves into a new will-unit in relation to that part of themselves which they surrender to the association. The *Anstalt* structure, on the other hand, appears when a single will injects part of itself into a group, thus unifying the group. In the former case there is formed ordinarily a corporation (*Körperschaft*), in the latter an institution (*Anstalt*) or a foundation (*Stiftung*)." *Die Genossenschaftstheorie* . . . , pp. 25-26.

The *Anstalt*, then, is created from above and resembles the "authoritarian union"; the *Genossenschaft* or *Körperschaft* is created from below or within a group.

just as real a unity of life in every human association which, by partially absorbing their individuality, binds a group of individuals together into a new and independent whole. For the significance of human existence could as little be created by a mere totaling of the lives (*Lebensinhalt*) of all individuals as it could be expressed by the picking out of single elements of associational life. Thus we find, above the level of individual existence, a second, independent level of existence of human collective associations. Above the individual spirit, the individual will, the individual consciousness, we recognize in thousand-fold expressions of life, the real existence of common spirit, common will, and common consciousness. And not figuratively, but in the most real sense of the word, we speak of "communities" (*Gemeinwesen*) over single individuals.[22]

Neither ruthless egoism nor passive subjection, says Gierke in another place, can characterize the relation between individual and group. Each exists for the other; neither may be considered purely as a means for realizing the purpose of the other. And the final goal by which individual and general purposes are to be measured ethically is the harmonious agreement of both.[23]

Human communal life is by no means concentrated in a single, universal form of association; the system of human association presents a complex picture of rich and fluid variety. Primitive associations based upon "purely physical" ties—the family, race, nation—give way to associations more consciously created and of more specialized function. The process of differentiation and specialization on the one hand is matched by a process of generalization on the other. Above restricted and simple associations appear higher, more inclusive associations, restricting, without absorbing, the activity and personality of the lesser.[24]

Below the united people there still exist the race, the *Gemeinde*, and the family, above it the international community of culture-peoples, and finally mankind in general, as narrower and wider human associational institutions with special spheres of life. . . . The ethical-social, the religious, the artistic and literary, the economic communal expe-

---

[22] "Die Grundbegriffe des Staatsrechts . . . ," pp. 301-302.
[23] "We seek the individual's purpose of life neither exclusively in himself nor exclusively in something outside himself. We predicate neither ruthless egoism nor unquestioning humility. But for us each lives for himself and at the same time for the whole. In their ultimate goals both seem to us to be one. Thus we never see the generality simply as an instrument for securing the ends of its members, but as a spontaneous higher moral purpose. Nor is the individual ever simply an instrument for the generality; but he finds his immediate purpose and worth in himself. But the ultimate goal by which we measure the moral justification of general as of individual purpose is the harmonious agreement of both." *Das deutsche Genossenschaftsrecht*, II, p. 42.
[24] "Die Grundbegriffe des Staatsrechts . . . ," p. 302.

riences all create, at different levels, their own special organisms, all of which have an independent existence as opposed to the state, whether they develop naturally or are consciously directed, whether they are formally proclaimed as unities or exist only as latent forces, whether they are as permanent as the state or as ephemeral as many clubs.[25]

As an expression of the social nature of man, the lowliest association shares original dignity and value with the highest and most comprehensive.

---

[25] *Ibid.*, p. 307.

CHAPTER V

At the apex of the system of higher and lower, of more and less inclusive associations, stands the state. From one point of view the state may be regarded as merely the highest and most inclusive association, homogeneous in nature with more restricted associations. It is the product of the same sort of forces as produce the *Gemeinde* or business corporation, and is "not generically different from them."

> We understand by "state" the highest and most inclusive among those collective entities, intangible but intellectually recognizable as "real," which human social existence erects above individual existence. For us this collective entity is the enduring, living, willing and acting unity formed by a whole folk.[1]

> Finally, the state, is of course, generality (*Allgemeinheit*), but it is by no means, as a widely published doctrine teaches, *simply human society*. It is only *one* among the associational organisms of mankind, and only one definite side of human social life is represented by it.[2]

> Stripped of its mystical character, considered in the light of its natural development instead of a supernatural origin, such a state is not generically different from the narrower communities of public law— from *Gemeinde* or corporation contained within it,—but it stands in relation to them only as the more perfect to the less perfect stage of development. It is the product of the same force that we see daily erecting generalities of a limited type. It is, therefore, homogeneous with the *Gemeinde* and the association.[3]

> It is but the last link in the chain of collective units developed into persons.[4]

To be sure, the state, like the *Gemeinde* and the commune, must have a territorial basis. But this is not sufficient to create a basic distinction between such political associations and other associations. An association to maintain dikes or a trade union of workers in a definite region may be equally territorial.[5]

---

[1] "Die Grundbegriffe des Staatsrechts . . . ," p. 175.
[2] *Ibid.*, p. 306.
[3] *Das deutsche Genossenschaftsrecht*, I, pp. 832-833.
[4] *Ibid.*, II, p. 831.
[5] *Cf. ibid.*, I, p. 833 and pp. 770 ff.

The state, then, is an association like the *Gemeinde*, the labor union, the joint-stock company, and so forth. So far we have a clear case for those who would interpret Gierke as a "pluralist,"[6] as a supporter of the view that "the state is only one among many forms of human association . . . not necessarily any more in harmony with the end of society than a church or a trade-union or a free-masons' lodge. . . ."[7] Such a view has undoubtedly been strengthened by the coincidence that it was Maitland who introduced Gierke to English-speaking academic circles. Being primarily an historian of the common law, Maitland's chief interest in Gierke was directed toward the private-law implications of Gierke's theory. Consequently he emphasized sharply Gierke's doctrine of the real personality of corporations, but paid little attention to the second basic principle of the *Genossenschaft*-theory—the organic nature and structure of all associations,—and practically no attention to the place of the state in Gierke's theory. Maitland was interested in Gierke's doctrines of the real personality, the independent origin, and the independent law and purpose of the association, and it is these things which lend support to the pluralistic conception of the relation of the state to lesser associations.

But so far we have heard but one side of Gierke's theory of the state; and overemphasis of this side has led to an exaggeration of the radical implications of Gierke's theory and a falsification of the theory itself. The state is an association. But it is also something more than a mere association, and at this point Gierke takes leave of the pluralists and follows the more beaten path of his German predecessors. For "the state is . . . the highest generality." "It is distinguished from all other collective persons in that it has no similar person above it."[8]

> Significant indeed is the series of consequences which flow from the single difference that the state as the highest generality has no generality above it; that it is sovereign; that while all other associations are determined by something outside themselves and find their ultimate regulating force outside themselves, the state alone is self-determined and bears its regulating force within itself.[9]

[6] *Cf.* Sobei Mogi, *Otto von Gierke*, pp. 117, 120.
[7] Harold Laski, *Authority in the Modern State*, p. 65.
[8] *Das deutsche Genossenschaftsrecht*, II, p. 831; *Die Genossenschaftstheorie* . . . , pp. 641-642; *cf. Das deutsche Genossenschaftsrecht*, II, p. 41.
[9] *Das deutsche Genossenschaftsrecht*, I, p. 833; *cf. Die Genossenschaftstheorie* . . . , pp. 152-153, 642.

The state, then, is distinguished from all other *Genossenschaf-ten* by the fact that it is the highest, most comprehensive organization—an organization having no controlling organization above it—in short, as Gierke puts it, a ' *sovereign*" association. The state, as the highest, most authoritative political organization, is distinguished also by its function of carrying out the "general will" and, consequently, by its duty of conciliating and coercing group wills of lesser associations. And, as such, its sphere of activity, which can not be defined once and for all, will project itself in some degree or other "into every sphere of human social life."[10]

As Emerson points out, Gierke offers no proof that his assumption agrees with facts at this point. "It seems evident that here Gierke is giving an artificial solution to the problem by means of definition," says Emerson; "in brief, that he is begging the question. The problem which must be solved is exactly whether the State, as we now know it, *is* universal, all-inclusive, and possessed of the highest power. Gierke's answer is that a territorial corporation which does possess all these qualities is a State, and is, in consequence, sovereign. The question as to whether such an all-inclusive and highest *Genossenschaft* exists in fact, as it does in the logical development of the *Genossenschaftstheorie,* appears not to have troubled him: he assumes its existence, calls it State, and sums up its qualities in the concept of sovereignty."[11] In expanding this criticism, we might ask with fairness just what is meant by "inclusive." Does the state include, at least partially, the pur-

---

Gierke sometimes phrases this point in a manner so emphatic as to suggest that the test of statehood is force. The following excerpt, for example, if standing alone, would certainly leave this impression:

"*Einen specifischen Charakter jedoch und eine Reihe qualitativer Unterschiede von allen anderen politischen Verbänden muss* derjenige *Machtverband aufweisen, dessen Macht nach oben hin durch keine ähnliche Macht beschränkt und nach unten hin jeder ähnlichen Macht überlegen ist. Denn eine Macht, welche die* höchste *ist, unterscheidet sich von jeder anderen Macht durch das specifische Merkmal, dass sie durch und durch Macht, die Macht schlechthin ist. . . ."* "Die Grundbegriffe des Staatsrechts . . .," p. 304.

But, translating *"Macht"* consistently as "authority," which, I believe, we must do in view of Gierke's repeated emphasis in other places upon the *Rechtstaat*, this passage merely strengthens what has been said above without substantially changing its meaning.

[10] "To be sure, the question of how far the domain of the state extends is not one to be fixed for all time, but depends upon the positive separation by time and circumstances of the political functions of life from the other social functions of life. But in some way or other, the problems and competence of political authority will always project themselves into *every* sphere of human social life. For in general the consideration of how far a general interest requires for its realization the authoritative (*machtvolle*) carrying out of the general will will always be decisive in bounding the political sphere. But to a certain point in all periods and in all cultural environments, all social functions, in order to develop fully and without hindrance, will be assigned to the protection and care of a power capable of coercing opposing wills. And so the state, even though theoretically it includes but one specific side of social life is . . . not an organization founded for a specific single purpose, but its functions correspond with the cultural functions of human society, because and in so far as a highest power (*Macht*) must exist for their realization." "Die Grundbegriffe des Staatsrechts . . . ." pp. 308-309. *Cf.* the discussion on pp. 85 ff., *infra.*

[11] Emerson, *State and Sovereignty in Modern Germany*, p. 138.

poses or ends of lesser associations, so that the "general will" is a composite will inclusive of lesser group wills? To put the point specifically, does the state as the universal association include such associations as the Catholic Church or an international steel cartel? Or can the state include, in any sense of the word, a section of the Third International?

But a second serious difficulty arises from Gierke's attempt to make the attribute of freedom from exterior determination and regulation the qualitative distinction of the state. Granted that certain aspects of the *Genossenschaft* must be submitted to the determination and regulation of the state—as their existence is recognized in law, and as their powers and even their internal structure may be defined from without—nevertheless, as Gierke has been at pains to show, the existence of the *Genossenschaft* as a living, willing person is only recognized and not determined by the state, and its purposes and effectual activity can not be reduced to what the state may allow.[12] In so far as the *Genossenschaft* determines its own purpose and real existence, does it not also possess a sphere—limited, it is true—in which its decision is ultimate? This *quantitative* difference in the ultimate authority of associated groups, which are all by nature "homogeneous," would seem logically to be the core of Gierke's *Genossenschaft*-theory; and on occasion Gierke himself seems to regard it as such. Yet when he comes to the state and its position in the system of associations, he transforms a quantitative distinction into a qualitative distinction—without, apparently, any recognition of inconsistency. Thus he introduces into his system an illogical twist which saves him from the radical conclusions reached by his follower, Preuss, who in his earlier writings insisted that the theoretical homogeneity between the state and other associations could lead only to a repudiation of the concept of state sovereignty.[13]

Gierke also attacks the problem from a different view and calls in the support of history when he points out that the state— or at least the historically-developed German state—was not a pure

---

[12] The law "can neither attribute personality to creatures of its own choice nor deny it arbitrarily." *Die Genossenschaftstheorie* . . . , p. 22; *v. supra*, p. 56 ". . . . The principle . . . of liberty . . . not only guarantees to the individual and other associations a certain sphere not to be disturbed by the state, but also guarantees a sphere of rights which are simply not to be touched by the state." "Die Grundbegriffe des Staatsrechts . . . ," p. 324. ". . . . The active powers of the social organism . . . realize their most powerful effects independently of law, or even in opposition to law." *Das Wesen der menschlichen Verbände*, p. 34.

[13] *Cf.* pp. 99 ff., *infra*.

association, but the creation of associational and authoritarian (*herrschaftlich*) elements. The basis of the modern state is the *Volksgenossenschaft*, or "the associational union of the collective folk," and, to the extent that the associational principle dominates in the modern state, authority rises from below. But unity and stability are added to the associational state by authority from above, and, in a sense, from without the association—specifically, from the monarchy. And form is given the modern constitutional state by an organic integration of the two elements—an integration which produces harmonious cooperation within a new organism.

> For although the *basis* of the modern constitutional state is formed by the idea of an associational union of the collective folk, that is, of a civil association in which all the fully and equally independent citizens are the active associates, yet its apex rises out of the *Herrschaft* principle transformed into princely authority. . . . Even the representative, constitutional state is . . . an entity in which an associational basis (the association of citizens) and an authoritarian apex (the monarchy) are bound together organically: that is, not as a mere sum, but as a new, living unity.[14]

The distinction between the state and lesser associations thus becomes very clearly a qualitative and not merely a quantitative distinction; and a qualitative distinction deeply rooted in the development of the German nation.

Futhermore, Gierke's recognition of the need for a single highest authority in the national community—a need recognized in the end by many of the pluralists[15]—appears to be reenforced by a patriotic respect and awful admiration for the Prussian monarchy that had done so much to weld the German people into a united nation. Gierke apparently became more and more convinced as time passed that the constitution of the Bismarckian *Reich* represented the closest approach to a perfect harmony between the associational and the authoritarian elements in the state. In more settled times, he, like Preuss, had demanded decentralizing reform which might be accomplished in the spirit of his *Genossenschaft*-theory; but in 1919 his fear of the disruption which must follow the with-

---

[14] *Das deutsche Genossenschaftsrecht*, I, p. 833; *cf.* also *Der germanische Staatsgedanke*, p. 7.

[15] *Cf.* F. Coker, "Pluralistic Theories and the Attack upon State Sovereignty," in Merriam and Barnes, *Political Theories, Recent Times*, especially pp. 95 ff.

drawal of the heavy hand of authority led him to vigorous and out-spoken criticism of the Weimar Constitution. The state organism, into which the monarchy has been woven as an integral part, must be preserved if the German nation is not to be destroyed. When he speaks bitterly in 1919, his state theory is still built upon the principles of his earlier writings, but the authoritarian principle has grown in importance until it seems to dwarf the antithesis it is supposed to balance.

> Our state shall remain an *organically* constructed community after the German pattern. As *Folk-state* it is to win a broader basis and a deeper anchorage in the consciousness of all classes of the Folk than it had before. But we shall do all that is within our power to prevent its surrender to the momentarily unorganized masses, or to a numerically superior class. We need a German *authority* (*Obrigkeit*), independent of the tendencies of the day and of party interest, which will guard the general and permanent interests of the whole Folk with a strong hand! The whole Folk, which is not simply a sum of casual individuals, but is a community consisting of head and members, binding present, past, and future generations in an undying unity of life. An independent government armed with its own authority and its own responsibility to protect us against impending anarchy and consequent disintegration through a violent dictatorship.[16]

---

[16] *Der germanische Staatsgedanke* (1919), p. 26.
It should be noted as a tribute to Gierke's sincere patriotism and intellectual integrity that the bulk of this last important lecture is not written in the highly emotional vein suggested by some of my quotations. Restating his own interpretation of the main lines of development in German political theory and institutions, *Der germanische Staatsgedanke* is a valuable addition to Gierke's writings. And as an index to Gierke's own personality it is equally significant. At eighty years of age, after the great tragedy of his life, he begins the study of a new German constitution which is as little to his liking as the revolution which produced it. Yet he speaks, for the most part, without bitterness and with a faith in the destiny of the German people which neither defeat nor revolution has been able to destroy completely.

CHAPTER VI

STATE, GENOSSENSCHAFT, AND LAW

Gierke's discussion of the origin of law in relation to the state is to a high degree anti-absolutist and anti-statist in tone, and would seem at first glance to give strong support to those who would challenge the sovereign authority of the state. Gierke would have none of the empty formalism of writers like Seydel, who defines law, in terms familiar to English and American lawyers, as "the regulatory principles laid down by the ruler for the rule."[1] One of the best statements of his own juristic theory grew out of a critical review devoted to the task of revealing the shallowness of the formalists who, content with their definitions, never penetrate beyond to the actual forces which create law.[2]

According to Gierke, the state does not create law; nor is the state anterior to law. Law and state are interdependent, but neither is superior to the other. The existence of state and law evidences two related but distinct sides of social life.

> Law is of equal birth with the state. It is as little drawn from the state as the state from it. But both, springing from independent roots, have developed together, to realize themselves only *through* each other. Like the idea of the state, the idea of law is, generally speaking, born with man.[3]

Being a *Rechtstaat,* the modern state, the German state for example, stands within law and recognizes legal limitations upon its own sovereign will. Being also a *Kulturstaat,* it does not restrict its activities merely to the preservation of the law, but "strives for the perfection of human society in *every* aspect."[4]

The state, to be sure, creates positive law, but it does not for that reason become the final source of law, nor even the sole enunciator of law. "The final source of all law remains the *social con-*

---

[1] *Cf.* "Die Grundbegriffe des Staatsrechts . . . ," p. 181.
[2] "Die Grundbegriffe des Staatsrechts. . . ."
[3] *Ibid.,* p. 310.
[4] *Ibid.,* pp. 313-314.

sciousness of any social institution whatever." (*"Letzte Quelle alles Rechtes vielmeher bleibt das* Gemeinbewusstsein *irgend einer socialen Existenz."*)[5] And the declaration which transforms a social conviction of right into law may take place through the state or through other agencies, such as church, family, *Gemeinde*.

> The social conviction that something is right needs, to be sure, embodiment through a social declaration in order to come into objective existence as a principle of law. But this declaration can take place in different ways. Usually, of course, it takes place through the state; it is a chief function of the *Kulturstaat* to formulate as law the consciousness of right of the people, and in many periods almost all other sources of law are suppressed by state law. Still beside the state operate in a similar and at times very far-reaching fashion other social organisms— for example, Church, family, *Gemeinde*, and so forth—as formative organs of law. And then there still remains in force, in addition to legislation and decree, the informal creation of law through custom, which originally prevailed throughout. In custom the common conviction of right comes to expression and thereby into objective existence as a doctrine of law through the direct activity of respective circles of associations. . . . From a subjective point of view, different categories of associations can be bearers of legal or political life. And so a politically disunited people can maintain the unity of their legal system; and within a single people can exist numerous special categories of law not necessarily coinciding with the political organization. And from the international community of nations, although it lacks state character, can arise international law.[6]

Law is not created solely by the state. Neither is it dependent upon force whether of the state or any other association. Without the ability to maintain itself by force, a state could not exist, says Gierke. But for the existence of law enforcement or lack of enforcement is irrelevant.

> While *force* is a theoretical assumption for the state, so that a state without every means of force would no longer be a state, it is irrelevant for the concept of law whether it has objective means of force at its command. Law, with or without means of enforcement, still remains *law*.[7]

---

[5] *Ibid.*, p. 310. Gierke's stand here comes close to that of Krabbe, who insists repeatedly that the obligatory force of all law resides in "man's common feeling or sense of right." But Gierke, of course, would reject Krabbe's conclusions that the state is simply a "legal community," and that "the authority of the state is nothing except the authority of law." *Cf.* H. Krabbe, *Modern Idea of the State*, tr. by Sabine and Shepard (1922).

[6] *Ibid.*, pp. 310-312.

[7] *Ibid.*, p. 312. *Cf.* "Recht und Sittlichkeit," in *Logos*, VI (1917).

Here again Gierke parts company with the formalists and follows his basic premises to their logical conclusion.

Out of Gierke's conception of the nature of the *Genossenschaft* grows a novel distinction in kinds of law. Corresponding to his division of persons into natural, individual persons and social, or collective persons, he finds a twofold basic division of law into "individual" and "social" law. "In accordance with the twofold nature of men, who are at the same time entities in themselves and parts of higher entities, law must be divided into two great branches, which we may designate as individual law and social law."[8]

The basic difference between the two branches of law is one which takes cognizance of the composite, organic nature of associations as contrasted with the individual, organic nature of individual persons. Law can regulate single individuals only externally; but "because and in so far as the inner structure of the social organism is at the same time the external life of men or more restricted societies of men," law can reach within the association and determine even the structure of the collective unit.[9] The legal concept of membership in the association, rights and duties pertaining to membership, the powers of the organs of the association, delimitation of the sphere of power of the association from the sphere remaining free to individual members—all these are matters demanding legal determinations.[10] The most distinguishing characteristic of social law, then, is the possibility (and necessity) of formulating into legal principles relations between the unitary whole and its individual parts—a concept utterly impossible in individual law. Since "societies share in common with single individuals the ability to exist as independent wholes and as members . . . of more inclusive units," social law must also deal with the construction of higher social organisms from lower; it must include principles for the integration, finally, of all into the "sovereign community."[11]

Speaking at an earlier date less philosophically and in more strictly juristic language,[12] Gierke makes his basic distinction one

---

[8] *Das Wesen der menschlichen Verbände*, pp. 26-27.
[9] *Ibid.*, p. 27.
[10] *Ibid.*, pp. 27-28.
[11] *Ibid.*, p. 31.
[12] "Die Grundbegriffe des Staatsrechts und die neuesten Staatsrechtstheorien" (1874). *Das Wesen der menschlichen Verbände* was first delivered as Gierke's *Rektorat* lecture in 1902. *Cf.* also *Die Genossenschaftstheorie* . . . , pp. 156 ff.; *Deutsches Privatrecht*, I, p. 27.

between "public" and "private" law. These categories are more narrow than those discussed above, but Gierke's terminology even here is not in strict accordance with the ordinary usage in jurisprudence, and his "public" law is' not to be confused with what we would call constitutional or state law.

Here Gierke explains that law is basically an "ordering of spheres of will." Since human will is divisible into individual will and common will, "so law must bear a specifically different character according to whether, as private law, it limits individual freedom of will, or, as public law, orders the common domain of will."[13] Private law sets up individuals as centers of individual spheres of will and considers associations as equivalent to individuals in so far as these enter into the private-law system of relations. But the individuals of private law are not treated as integrated parts of higher units; their relations to other individuals are regarded merely as "mechanical attachments between closed units of life." "The kernel of private law is the setting up of a free sphere of activity in which the individual creates legal relations through his own free act of will."[14]

Public law, on the other hand, treats, not of individuals, but of groups or members of groups.

> Public law knows no isolated individuals, but only groups or members of groups. Instead of a world of coordinated and self-encompassed units of will, it postulates a world of social beings in which from the beginning will is determined by its organic relations to other wills; in which the composite unity of the whole is referred to the multiplicity of single wills and the multiplicity of single units referred to the unity of the general will; in which, through the simultaneous recognition of the common personality of the whole and the member personality of the individuals, there is set up immediately a qualitative gradation of legal entities, a twofold system of will.[15]

The boundary between the two laws is, of necessity, fluid. Just where a grouping of individuals ceases to be bound together by simply "a complex of mechanical individual relationships," and forms a composite organism, must frequently be determined by positive law with some degree of arbitrary judgment. Moreover, the same collective unit may appear to its own members as a public-

[13] "Die Grundbegriffe des Staatsrechts . . . ," p. 315.
[14] Ibid., p. 316.
[15] Ibid.. p. 317.

law unit, but to those outside its sphere of control as a subject of private law. A church, for example, could be regarded by its own members only as a public-law association, but, from without its own membership, it might conceivably be regarded as both a public-law and a private-law person.[16]

I have already said that Gierke's public law is not to be confused with state law or constitutional law. State law, however, is one branch of law which is "simply, absolutely, and for all purposes public law." For state law is that law which includes the state as generality and all individuals and other groups as members of the state.[17] Gierke's treatment of state law in relation to other public law is similar to and consistent with his treatment of the state in relation to other associations—and is, therefore, open to the same criticism. State law has a place at the peak, certainly, but still *within* the system of public law. From one point of view, state-law concepts are but enlargements upon a higher plane of concepts applicable in descending degree for all associations down to the lowest.

> As the state always remains simply the highest among human associations and similar to them in the general characteristics of an associational organism, so state law has a position at the peak, to be sure, but within the general system of public associational law. For this reason, all state-law concepts may be viewed as enlargements of corresponding corporation concepts, and the internal structure of state law is analogous to that of corporation law. Therefore there belongs to the totality of public law a system of thought which repeats itself in very unequal fullness and significance from the lowest steps of organic union up to the state. . . .[18]

But a qualitative distinction similar to that between state and lower associations must now be added to this quantitative difference.

> . . . . There exists no legally organized generality for which the state could be a mere particular. State law is, therefore, different from all other public associational law in the same manner as the state itself differs from other collective entities. In so far as the specific nature of the state as a sovereign association comes under consideration, there must be set forth a special interpretation of every concept and institution.[19]

---

[16] *Ibid.*, pp. 317-319.
[17] *Ibid.*, p. 319.
[18] *Ibid.*, p. 319.
[19] *Ibid.*, p. 319.

> The state, elevated over all by its sovereign complete power, lays claim to a law of a higher order, and permits only such communities as it considers to be public establishments to take part to a certain degree in the prerogatives of public law.[20]

State law, the law of the highest and most inclusive association, is qualitatively different from the law of lesser associations, just as the state is, in the end, qualitatively different from lower associations.

Certain associations, in so far as they occupy an intermediate position between state and citizen, may share in this special law of the state. But their position necessitates a greatly extended control by the state over their structure, power, and activity.

> In so far as a corporation is considered generally or for certain purposes as only a special entity as opposed to the state, its public-law position in the state will be equal or analogous to that of single citizens. But special legal relations enter in so far as a corporation is considered as a more restricted community for the state as an *intermediate organism* between the state whole and single citizens. For here it becomes necessary to draw a line between the two capacities of the narrower association—that of being an entity for itself and that of being a member of the state. So it becomes necessary with such an association to distinguish not only between the private-law and public-law sides of personality but further, within the public-law sphere, between the collective significance of this personality for itself and its significance as a member of the state. So far as the member-position of the narrower association reaches, the state will possess a more or less extended right over, not only the external, but also the *internal* life of the organism attached to it. The rise and modification, composition, business, content and compass of membership, its organization and activity in general will not be determined for the narrower community by its will alone, but to some degree or other by the will of the state.[21]

Here again the idea of an organically integrated national community permeated by the ever-present sovereignty of the all-inclusive state seems to qualify strongly the implications of Gierke's basic postulates.

In a discussion of Gierke's legal theory Georg Gurwitch makes the following judgment: "Gierke's great achievement, which can not be too highly valued, has been his breaking away from the

---

[20] *Das Wesen der menschlichen Verbände*, p. 32. Here "public law" is to be understood in the conventional sense.

[21] "Die Grundbegriffe des Staatsrechts . . . ," pp. 326-327.

hypnosis of modern conditions in his theoretical distinction between the two fields of law and his definition of social law in
terms independent of the state concept."[22] The same writer then
maintains that Gierke's theory of social law, "the most realistic
and forward-looking of present theories of law," furnishes a theoretical basis for the numerous pluralistic and federalistic tendencies represented by such writers as Duguit, Hauriou, Hobson and
the Gild Socialists, Russell, and Rathenau.[23] Gierke's statement of
the origin of law, his statement of the relation of state and law,
and his definition of social law may open a new and interesting
approach to the pluralist and the radical federalist. But an interpretation of these phases of Gierke's theory which fails to take into
account the special position of Gierke's state and state law is
scarcely an accurate interpretation of Gierke.

[22] "Otto von Gierke als Rechtsphilosoph," in *Logos*, XI (1922-1923), p. 130.
[23] *Ibid.*, pp. 131-132.

CHAPTER VII

FEDERAL ASPECTS OF THE GENOSSENSCHAFT-THEORY

There now remain for discussion the elements of federalism involved in the *Genossenschaft*-theory, and Gierke's recognition and handling of the relation between *Genossenschaft* and federalism.

It is worthy of notice that Gierke finds in those historical periods in which the *Genossenschaft* idea seemed to dominate social organization a strong tendency toward federalism in theory, and even, to a limited extent, in practice. The medieval period, during which the dominant form of organization was the "free union" (*Einung*), was also a period during which organization and social theory seemed to turn naturally towards federalism. While medieval thought proceeded from the whole, still it conceded always to each more restricted unit a life, purpose, and value of its own. And the universal whole was never conceived as absolute or exclusive, but formed only "the spire of an organically integrated social structure."

> When truly medieval thought postulated the visible unity of mankind in Church and Empire, still it narrowed this unity *to such relations* as the *common purpose of mankind demanded*. It is, therefore, neither absolute nor exclusive, but forms only the spire of an organically integrated social structure. In Church and State the collective bodies fell into place as graduated member bodies, each of which required connection with the whole, but at the same time created for itself a whole endowed with a special purpose and organized within itself according to the principles of plurality and ruling unity. Between the highest generality and the inalienable unity of the individual a series of intermediary unities are introduced, each of which draws together and embraces the unities of a narrower circle. Medieval theory strives to create a fixed scheme for this organization. . . .[1]

"So there resulted the thoroughly federalistic structure of the social whole, in harmony with the medieval manner of life,"[2] in

---

[1] *Das deutsche Genossenschaftsrecht*, III, pp. 544-545; *cf.* practically the same statement in *Johannes Althusius* . . . , p. 226.
[2] *Johannes Althusius* . . . , p. 226.

which the *Genossenschaft* "strove to set up with other *Genossenschaften* a wider association to which, as a member of a higher generality, it voluntarily surrendered part of its own independence."[3] It is exactly this "federalistic construction of the social world" which was gradually destroyed by the new "antique-modern" concept of state centralization and absolutism.[4]

More specific realization of the federal principle, which arose naturally from the principle of free union, Gierke found in the numerous city leagues of the thirteenth to fifteenth centuries.[5] And a federal organization from below of the feudal Empire was only prevented by the exclusion of the peasant class from the associational movement.[6]

> Indeed, more than once the free union was close to the point of rewinning, by the path of federalism, the unity of the Empire itself, a unity which had been lost with the sundering of feudal bonds. And what finally was saved of Empire unity at the end of the fifteenth century was saved simply by force of the principle of free union.[7]

> Out of merchant gilds and city leagues arose the great commercial republic of the north. Federal leagues of cities came to life in all parts of the Empire, and led the political movement towards unity. Leagues of princes, nobles and knights, unions of prelates and clerics followed in the same path. The Estates among themselves sought to realize in leagues of peace a higher system of law. More than once did the final goal of the free union, the goal of a federal union of the Empire, approach realization; and, if political unity of the Empire was not achieved, an Empire-unit with certain political functions was at least saved.[8]

The final blow against what survived of this medieval federalistic pluralism in the seventeenth century was struck by the natural-law philosophy which tended to set the naked, unattached individual against the sovereign state and to seek justification for and limitation of his subjection in the social contract. But among the natural-law writers Gierke finds one of particular interest, because, through the social contract, he reconstructs from the bottom up the sort of social organization which during the medieval period had always been constructed from the top down. Althusius

[3] *Das deutsche Genossenschaftsrecht*, I, p. 299.
[4] *Ibid.*, III, p. 545.
[5] *Cf.* pp. 32-33, *supra*.
[6] *Cf.* p. 33, *supra*.
[7] *Das deutsche Genossenschaftsrecht*, I, p. 299.
[8] *Ibid.*, I, p. 582.

does not attempt to clear the field of all intermediate associations and limit the authority of the state only as against individuals; rather he builds up the state through a hierarchy of lesser associations. As a consequence, Gierke is able to state: "Among all the original characteristics of the political system of Althusius, none is perhaps so startling as the spirit of *federalism* which prevades it from head to foot."[9] Gierke gives in a single sentence an admirably concise summary of the federalistic structure of Althusius' system:

> So there resulted for him a pure natural-law social structure in which family, vocational association, *Gemeinde,* and province stood as necessary and organic members (*Gliederungen*) between the individual and the state; in which the wider association was always constructed from the corporate union of narrower associations; . . . in which each narrower association, as a true and spontaneous (*originäres*) community, created of itself a special community life and its own sphere of rights, and of these surrendered to the higher association only as many as this higher association required for fulfilling its specific purpose; in which, finally, the state, in all else, is generically similar to its member associations and differs from them only in its exclusive sovereignty, which, as the highest earthly legal power, acquires a multitude of new and peculiar attributes and functions, but finds an impassible barrier in the original right of the narrower associations, with the passing of which barrier it becomes void, since, through the breach of the compact of union, the members recover their right to full sovereignty.[10]

Gierke was apparently strongly influenced by his study of the medieval German association and by his rediscovery of Althusius; and it can not be denied that his theory of the *Genossenschaft* has much in common with what he describes as the medieval social theory and with the system of Althusius. To be sure, there are significant differences. Gierke can not rely upon a divine reason

---

[9] *Johannes Althusius* . . . , p. 226.
[10] *Ibid.,* p. 244. Notice also the following selection on Althusius from *Das deutsche Genossenschaftsrecht*: "It was *Johannes Althusius* who reduced to a single principle the federalistic ideas afloat in his religious and political circles, and worked them into an intelligently conceived system. *Althusius* insisted that the attribute of sovereignty provided a sharp theoretical distinction between the state and every other community . . . . Nevertheless, while he bound the *majestas* by legal restrictions, although he declared it to be the highest earthly power, and while considering it unitary, indivisible, and inalienable, still refused to see in it the exclusive embodiment of the authority . . . residing in human associations, he thus reserved for narrower associations an original sphere of law and an original position in the structure of civil society. To this extent he came close to the original system of thought of the Middle Ages. But while medieval federalism proceeded from the unity of the whole *Althusius* proceeded from the basis of natural-law. individualism and deduced all social unity from organization built up from below. . . . [Intermediate associations] did not lead a communal life loaned them by the state, but one arising from themselves, . . . so that while they could exist without the state, the state could not exist without them." *Das deutsche Genossenschaftsrecht,* IV, pp. 345-347.

and order to insure harmony within the universe. Nor can he attribute any validity to the contract theory of the origin of associations. But his *Genossenschaft* has traits very similar to those of the medieval *Einung* or Athusius' *consociatio*. For Gierke the *Genossenschaft* is a spontaneous association, possessed of its own personality and of its own sphere of will, action, and law. It is capable of organic integration into higher or more inclusive associations whose members are individuals or associations; but such integration can not, without destroying Gierke's theory, involve absorption. In any organization into a wider generality the independent personality and the original sphere of will, action, and law of the lesser association must be safeguarded. Now if the social whole is to be constructed upon the basis of ever-widening unions of such associations, culminating for the present in the inclusive state, it would seem that the whole structure would of necessity have to be conceived as a federalistic structure. Such was the structure of medieval theory and of Althusius, and such, it seems to me, should be the conclusion of a logical development of Gierke's principal premises. Such a federalistic structure might even be made compatible with state sovereignty if, as in Althusius' system, the sovereign power of the state "finds an impassible barrier in the original rights of narrower associations." To what extent does Gierke recognize or admit the existence of such a necessary connection between his *Genossenschaft*-theory and federalism?

In the first place, it may be pointed out that Gierke's *Genossenschaft*-theory, applied to the question of *Bundesstaat,* made possible a unique solution of the problem of the juristic construction of the old *Reich*. To the volumes of dispute on the subject,[11] Gierke added one article in which through the *Genossenschaft*-principle he was able to retain the concept of individual sovereignty without sacrificing the autonomous personality of either central or member states.[12]

In this well-known review of Laband, Gierke maintains the impossibility of discovering between the member states of a federal state and the communal members (*Gemeinde*, communes) of

---

[11] For a summary of German theories of federalism before 1870, see Gierke's *Johannes Althusius* . . . , Ch. V, and Siegfried Brie, *Der Bundesstaat: eine historisch-dogmatische Untersuchung* (1874). The best concise summary of nineteenth century German theories of federalism is Emerson, *op. cit.,* Ch. III.

[12] "Labands Staatsrecht und die deutsche Rechtswissenschaft," in (Schmoller's) *Jahrbuch für Gesetzgebung, Verwaltung und Volkswirtschaft,* VII (1883), pp. 1097-1195. This is a review of Laband, *Das Staatsrecht des deutschen Reiches,* Vol. III, Part 2 (1882).

the unified state a clear qualitative distinction on the basis of which
state personality may be attributed to the former but not to the
latter. If writers like Laband and Jellinek,[13] while insisting upon
maintaining the theory of sovereignty, repudiate Waitz' simple
solution of dividing sovereignty (or *Staatsgewalt*) between central and member states, what test then remains to distinguish the
non-sovereign member state? Gierke can not accept Laband's
explanation that the distinguishing feature is the possession by the
member state of its own "original right to public-law authority."[14]
For what, after all, is "original right" (*eigenes Recht*)? If it
is simply right not derived from the central government, then not
only *Gemeinde* and communes but even many corporations share
this characteristic with the member state—and the characteristic
ceases to be distinctive.[15] Finally, Gierke considers the suggestion
that the test of the member state in distinction from communal
units is "the content of its sphere of power." But even here there
is no real distinction because "not a single power can be cited as
natural to a member state which could not also appear as the power
of a corporation."[16]

To Gierke, then, it seems almost a fruitless labor to attempt
an abstract distinction between the member state of a *Bundesstaat*
and the communal member of a unitary state. As a jurist, he can
not find a satisfactory distinction; but, even as a jurist, he can
not brush aside a difference which exists in fact. For it is obvious
that in the course of history certain collective units appear as
states and others do not.[17]

The way towards a satisfactory construction of the *Bundesstaat*
is, according to Gierke, that pointed out by Hänel when he maintained "that in the *Bundesstaat* the full state appears not in the
central state and not in the member states, but in the *totality* of
the two."[18] Gierke starts with the assumption of state sovereignty,
which he finds to be supported by "the legal knowledge of modern
peoples." He accepts the further usual assumption of the indivis-
ibility of sovereignty. If, then, legal theory recognizes several subjects of state power, or sovereignty, in the same community, this

---

[13] *Cf.* George Jellinek. *Die Lehre von den Staatenverbindungen* (1882).
[14] "Labands Staatsrecht," p. 67 (p. 1163).
[15] *Ibid.*, pp. 67-68 (pp. 1163-1164). *Cf.* other arguments against this concept, pp. 67-69.
[16] *Ibid.*, p. 70 (p. 1166).
[17] *Ibid.*, pp. 70-71 (pp. 1166-1167).
[18] *Ibid.*, p. 71 (p. 1167); *cf.* Hänel, *Studien* (1873), I, pp. 63 ff.

can only mean that a plurality of subjects is in possession of the body of rights and duties which constitutes sovereignty. "Therefore, in the *Bundesstaat* the *state-power* as such is formed exactly as in the unitary state. The difference lies simply in the peculiar formation of the *subject* of the state-power, which is here not a single collective person, but a plurality of collective persons bound together in a definite manner."[19] This combination which is the subject of sovereign authority includes the central state and member states organized into an organic union.

> Obviously only the *plurality (Mehrheit) of existent state-persons in their organic unity* can be considered the subject of the state power which is in substance indivisible. The collective state and the single states in their union form the subject which becomes a single personality. This organic association is not a new state *person* above its parts. For it lacks any special organization and its own organs. On the other hand, it may not be considered as simply the *sum* of existent state persons. For it is only in a definite constitutional union, by virtue of which they are permanently joined together and made interdependent, that the single states have a share in it. Its organic character is especially apparent in the fact that within itself it is a membered whole. The position of the members is not one of equality; for the central state as such is the *head* of the union. For this reason the collective state represents the collectivity of members externally, and has also the last word in internal disputes. In this way the necessary unity of the personality is preserved, and in spite of the division of legal state subjectivity in a multiple personality, in the last instance, the unity of the will of the state is guaranteed.[20]

Undivided sovereignty is thus retained in the *Bundesstaat* by attributing it to a plurality of subjects organically united into an association. And the member states, as well as the central state, may claim state personality because, through their constitutional relation to the collective state, they share in the possession of the total sovereign power of the state.

> Thus it becomes clear why in the *Bundesstaat* the whole, and, similarly, the parts are really *state* persons. They are such because, subordinated to no higher person, they are the bearers of the unitary state sphere of power the exercise of which is divided among them. The member states especially would not appear as "states" either on ac-

[19] "Labands Staatsrecht," p. 72 (p. 1163).
[20] *Ibid.*, pp. 72-73 (pp. 1168-1169); *cf.* also *Das deutsche Genossenschaftsrecht*, II, p. 854.

count of their rights of membership within the sovereign collective personality nor on account of their particular right within their own non-sovereign spheres, were they not at the same time construed in consti-tutional relationship to the collective state as sharing in the total sovereign power of the state.[21]

A private-law analogy for this construction may be found in the concept of the common property of a corporation. If the total property of a corporation is to be regarded as indivisible, then the rights of ownership may not be assigned to the corporate juristic person to the exclusion of its individual members, nor to the individual members to the exclusion of the juristic person. The rights of ownership must be assigned to the collective person and single members in common.[22] This concept of common property is but the objective corollary of the subjective concept of the *Genossenschaft*, which has already been discussed in detail.

With such a conception of the *Bundesstaat*, Gierke had no other alternative than to classify the Bismarckian *Reich* as *Bundesstaat*. The new *Reich*, he tells us in 1874, must be classified as a "consti-tutional-Monarchical *Bundesstaat*."[23] Like the old *Reich*, the new *Reich* is a *Bundesstaat* because it is "a composite political organism in which the state sphere is so *divided* between the central state representing the whole and the single states which form the members, that *full* statehood appears only in the organic articulation of both."[24]

But it is quite evident that Gierke did not regard a *bundes-staatlich* (*i.e.*, federal, in the usual political and juristic sense) organization of the *Reich* as either necessary or entirely desirable. It is quite evident also that he did not regard the *Bundesstaat* as a necessary corollary of the application of the *Genossenschaft* principle to state organization. In the first volume of *Das deutsche Genossenschaftsrecht*, published in 1868, Gierke expressed the

[21] "Labands Staatsrecht." pp. 73-74 (np. 1169-1170).
    Application of this theory of the *Bundesstaat* to the present baffling problem of juristically construing the British Commonwealth of Nations might give interesting illustra-tion of the ingenuity of Gierke's solution.
[22] *Ibid.*, pp. 74-75 (pp. 1170-1171).
[23] "Das alte und das neue deutsche Reich," in Fr. von Holtzendorff and W. Oncken, *Deutsche Zeit- und Streit-fragen*, III, 35 (1874), p. 15.
[24] *Ibid.*, p. 16. In discussing the point further, Gierke says: "Undoubtedly the *new Reich* is a true *Bundesstaat*, for, on the one hand, the member states retain their state nature; on the other hand, by a voluntary commitment 'for all time' they have set up a collective state as a state-creature of a higher order above them—a collective state which rests independent and powerful upon itself, which is for itself purpose, and which governs with the plenitude of state power not only the united single states but also every individual German directly." *Ibid.*, p. 17.

opinion that the united German state could only develop into a unitary state. This was necessarily true because of the monarchic form of the German states and because of the predominance of Prussia. He was convinced that, if unity were to be achieved, the member states could no longer continue as "states within a state."

> As the legal nature of the present German state structure is hard to define because it is a mixture of confederate, federal, and unitary elements, so the direction of its future development can be neither towards a confederate nor a federal state, but only towards a unitary *Reich*. A true association of states (*Staatengenossenschaft*) among monarchic states is, generally speaking, difficult to conceive; among a group of states in which one is greater than the sum of all the rest it is impossible. Here the only possibility is a real unitary state in which a centralized and an associational basis built from the collectivity of *Reich* citizens are united into a single collective state organism. In such a *Reich* there remains for the single states, if they are not to assume an unorganic position, only the significance of territorial unions standing between state and *Gemeinde*. . . . If the *united* German state is to be realized, they must cease to be states within states. . . .[25]

But we have already seen that this brave prediction did not deter Gierke from recognizing six years later that, for the time at least, the union established was a federal union.[26]

Just as his desperate devotion to the monarchy came to strongest expression when he saw the Prussian and imperial throne begin to totter, so his insistence upon the necessity of Prussian dominance was most forceful when he saw the unity and control of Prussia threatened.

> It is scarcely necessary to point out that there could be no graver sin against Germany's future than the destruction or mutilation of the Prussian state. Of this single great state of Germany, which alone is in a position permanently to protect the German nature (*Wesen*), towards the east against slavery, towards the west against the Gallic world! Of this proven source of political leadership, without which the nation must ever be denied restoration to power and greatness![27]

In recapitulation of what has been said so far, we may say that, although the *Genossenschaft*-theory facilitated the difficult

---

[25] *Das deutsche Genossenschaftsrecht*, I, p. 842.
[26] The classification of the Bismarckian *Reich* is prefaced by the following statements: "From the point of view of its legal nature, the new *Reich* as a *constitutional monarchic Bundesstaat* has no equal among the existing states of the world. All other constitutional monarchies are unitary states; all other *Bundesstaaten* are republics." "Das alte und das neue deutsche Reich," pp. 15-16.
[27] *Der germanische Staatsgedanke*, in *Staat, Recht und Volk*, No. 5 (1919), p. 25.

task of finding a juristically suitable construction for the *Reich* as *Bundesstaat,* Gierke apparently saw no necessary connection between *Bundesstaat* and the *Genossenschaft*-theory. Before 1870 he was apparently convinced that the German *Reich* could develop only as a unitary state. Yet he believed also that the *Reich* should be reformed internally in accordance with *Genossenschaft* principles.

We find some clue to Gierke's conception of what a *genossenschaftlich* reconstruction of the *Reich* would imply in the following quotation:

> If the *united* German state is to be realized, the single German states must cease to be states within a state. This means, however, that they must give up only the nature of *fully sovereign states,* not the state quality generally. For they shall not stand alone as communities homogeneous with the state, arising from themselves and limited only in the interest of central unity, but, in the form of associational collective units, provinces and districts (*Kreise*) even down to the *Ortgemeinde* will take their place as similar communities. If the realization of the *united* state demands greater limitation upon the single states, the realization of the *free* state necessitates, on the other hand, the greater independence of the narrower and wider communal units.[28]
>
> In accordance with its nature, the *Gemeinde* must be recognized as an *associational community* which, viewed from below, is generality, and, viewed from above, is part of a higher generality, and in relation to individuals is an individual. Just as the *Gemeinde* can not become again a medieval state within a state, neither can it remain a state institution with a borrowed juristic personality. . . . In public law the same *Gemeinde*-personality is, on the one hand, a member of a higher organism—above all, of the state; in this relation its position corresponds with that of the individual citizen. But, on the other hand, it is, for its own members, generality, and, as such, the source of a *public law* which controls their special spheres, and the possessor of *public power* of its own.[29]

Not only the member state, but also the province, the *Gemeinde,* and even the local commune must be recognized as occupying organic positions at different levels within the state whole. The *Genossenschaft* principle must replace the authoritarian principle. The reorganization of the system of local administration "must

---

[28] *Das deutsche Genossenschaftsrecht,* I, p. 843.
[29] *Ibid.,* I, p. 759.

proceed upon the basis of the essential equality (*Ebenburtigkeit*) of state and *Gemeinde*."[30]

One point, the central point in Gierke's thought on this, as on other subjects, can not be overemphasized. The decentralization which he considered a necessary administrative reform was not to come as a devolution of power from the authoritarian state to lesser units. Decentralization was to take the form rather of the recognition of autonomous spheres of authority already in the possession of lesser units by their own right. A *genossenschaftlich* organization, then, whether it exist within the *Bundesstaat* or the decentralized unitary state, would of necessity be of a federal nature. "Federal" in a non-juristic sense[31] and "*genossenschaftlich*" become almost synonymous; but not entirely, because of the exclusive sovereignty of the state.

So far we may go without violating Gierke's own interpretation of his system. What can be said now of the position in the *genossenschaftlich* political structure of the business corporation, the trade union, the sports club, and so on? Gierke has already attributed to many of these practically the same attributes as those possessed by *Gemeinde,* province, or commune. Are they too to take their places as organic members of the political whole? It is very interesting to observe that Gierke uses the similarity in nature between corporation and political-territorial associations negatively to break down the juristic distinctions set up by other writers, but in his own system tends always to differentiate rather sharply between political and non-political associations. The state, as the highest political association, is distinguished by possession of highest power or authority. It apparently is distinguished also by its function of carrying out "the general will." It has therefore the duty of conciliating and coercing special group wills of lesser associations.[32] The political sphere is thus marked off from other spheres in the manner and to the extent that "the political functions of life" are marked off from "other social functions of life."

[30] *Ibid.*, I, p. 714. *Cf.* also *ibid.*, I, pp. 710 ff., and Preuss' discussion of the *Genossenschaft*-theory in relation to administrative reform: "Die Lehre Gierkes und das Problem der preussischen Verwaltungsreform," in *Festgabe der Berliner juristischen Fakultät für Otto Gierke zum Doktor-Jubilaum, 21 August, 1910,* I (1910). Preuss points out that Gierke furnishes a theoretical basis for the movement towards administrative decentralization initiated by Stein at the beginning of the nineteenth century and later buried under the more powerful movement towards unification and centralization.
[31] See pp. 7-8. *supra.*
[32] *Cf.* "Die Grundbegriffe des Staatsrechts . . . ," pp. 308-309.

And, presumably, lesser political associations can share this distinctive position of the state on lower levels of authority.

On the other hand, Gierke has said that the state is the final, all-inclusive association. By "inclusive" he does not mean "absorptive." But does he mean inclusive, partially at least, of the purposes or ends of lesser associations? The following quotation from "Die Grundbegriffe des Staatsrechts" would seem to suggest that he does mean this:

> . . . . The living *political* element of all other social as individual entities finds its final definition of purpose and definitive boundary in the state. . . . To be sure, the question of how far the domain of the state reaches is not one to be fixed for all time, but depends upon the positive separation by time and circumstances of the political functions of life from the other social functions of life. But, in some way or other, the problems and competence of political authority will always project themselves into *every* sphere of human social life. For in general the consideration of how far a general interest requires for its realization the authoritative (*machtvolle*) carrying out of the general will will always be decisive in bounding the political sphere. But to a certain point in all periods and in all cultural environments, all social functions, in order to develop fully and without hindrance, will be assigned to the protection and care of a power capable of coercing opposing wills. And so the state, even though theoretically it includes but one specific side of social life, is, according to its reason for existence, not an organization founded for a specific single purpose, but its functions correspond with the cultural functions of human society, because and in so far as a highest power must exist for their realization.[33]

If the end or purpose of the state is conceived as composite and inclusive of what is common in the ends of "ethical, religious, artistic, literary, economic" associations, then should such associations not be bound into the state structure upon the same basis as are purely political associations? In other words, should the federalism implicit in the system not be a functional as well as a political-territorial federalism? The idea suggested in the above quotation Gierke does not develop in specific detail, and the possibility of a functional federalism he does not even suggest.

We may say, in conclusion, that Gierke saw as a necessary corollary to his *Genossenschaft*-theory as applied to the state a type of decentralization which closely approaches political federal-

---

[33] *Ibid.*, pp. 308-309.

ism, but that this decentralization was not necessarily tied up with the form of *Bundesstaat*; that he found a sufficient distinction between political and non-political associations to exclude the latter from the same "organic" position in the state structure which he demanded for the former; and, finally, that he was willing to sacrifice neither unity under Prussian dominance nor monarchy for the realization of his decentralized ideal, and consequently, the element of authoritarianism became increasingly dominant and the federal tendency increasingly weaker as the times became more desperate and Gierke himself increased in conservatism.

CHAPTER VIII

CRITICAL SUMMARY

I. I have pointed out that Gierke's dogmatic conclusions are based to a considerable extent upon suggestions which he draws from his historical interpretations. In his generalizations, derived from a mass of detailed evidence, one can not but notice in Gierke a tendency toward rather vague philosophical conclusions and a tendency also to idealize—*i.e.,* to transform into ideological or spiritual movements—social movements and social forces.[1] A judgment upon the validity of such generalizations can be made only by one who has worked his way through at least a considerable portion of the material which Gierke considers in the four volumes of *Das deutsche Genossenschaftsrecht.* We can, therefore, only draw attention here to criticisms of Gierke's historical interpretations by Rudolph Sohm and by George von Below. Sohm objects particularly to Gierke's identification in old-German law of the state concept and the *Genossenschaft* concept, and of public authority and associational authority.[2] In reply to this objection, Gierke pointed out the danger, often emphasized by Maitland also, of reading into the obscure past the sharp distinctions of modern jurisprudence. "In their effort to give the most clearly delineated picture of the past, many legal historians fall into the error of reading into the fluid concept of state and law of the German past the sharply formulated categories of modern juristic dogma."[3] Von Below criticizes what he considers to be Gierke's overemphasis of the influence of the *Einung* (free union) during the late feudal period. The *Herrschaft* element, the element of lordship or authority, is more important than Gierke is willing to allow, says von Below. Objecting to the interpretation emphasized by Gierke, De Wulf maintains that thirteenth century political thought was

---

[1] *Cf.* especially *Das deutsche Genossenschaftsrecht,* I, Introduction.
[2] Rudolph Sohm. *Die altdeutsche Reiches und Gerichtsverfassung,* I (Freiburg, 1871); *cf.* summary in Georg von Below, *Der deutsche Staat des Mittelalters,* I (Leipzig, 1914), pp. 52 ff.
[3] *Das deutsche Genossenschaftsrecht,* II, p. 5, n. 1.

dominated by the philosophical conception of the value of the individual. The unity of the group, De Wulf asserts, was understood as a unity of order only, and the group had no purpose that was not a means to the fulfillment of individual ends.[4] For our purposes, however, it is fortunately not necessary to attempt an evaluation of Gierke's historical conclusions. Our interest in this historical material lies simply in Gierke's interpretation of it as the background for his own system of theory.

In his recent edition of Althusius, Professor Friedrich maintains that the most important shortcoming of Gierke's study of Althusius is the failure sufficiently to emphasize the distinction between the sociological or political field—with which Althusius was primarily concerned—and the legal. By discussing Althusius' system as though it were a public-law system, Gierke creates a false impression of Althusius, says Friedrich.[5] Friedrich also challenges Gierke's characterization of the Althusian system as "federal"; but by "federalism" Friedrich means "that form of political life which is organized in a federal state." He would prefer to designate Althusius' aim as simply "decentralization."[6]

II. As Maitland has shown, Gierke's development of the implications of his association-theory for the legal position of corporations was a most significant contribution to modern jurisprudence.[7] In deriving law from "the general consciousness of right" and in pointing out that its formulation was not necessarily dependent on the state, Gierke elaborated a conception which not only served his *Genossenschaft*-theory, but also based jurisprudence upon empirical fact and secured its ethical dignity.

It becomes obvious from even a cursory examination of Gierke's writing that his main interest, aside from his interest in historical research, was not in political theory but in jurisprudence, and particularly in corporation law. His political theory is really but a by-product of other interests. Consequently the implications of certain phases of his political theory are left without satisfactory explanations. As a result of this, we search in vain for clear, un-

---

[4] Below, *op. cit.*, pp. 261 ff.; Maurice De Wulf, "L'Individu et le Groupe dans la Scolastique du XIIIᵉ Siècle," in *Revue Néo-Scolastique de Philosophie*, XXII (1920), pp. 341-358; for the criticisms of other writers see Below, pp. 88-90.
[5] C. J. Friedrich, *Politica Methodice Digesta of Johannes Althusius* (1932), pp. lxiii ff.
[6] *Ibid.*, p. lxxxvii.
[7] In addition to Maitland's Introduction to Gierke, *Political Theories of the Middle Ages*, see Pollock, "Has the Common-Law Received the Fiction Theory of Corporations?" in *Festschrift Otto Gierke zum siebzigsten Geburtstag* (1911).

equivocal definitions on several important points, such as the
meaning of "political," the distinction between categories of association, the federalistic structure implicit in the theory; and we are
left to deduce Gierke's views on such points from his general position. This opens the way to confused interpretations, and makes it
possible for members of widely divergent schools of thought to
call upon Gierke's authority in support of their own views.

III. Returning now to the specific questions stated in my introduction, I should say that this study has led to the following
conclusions:

Gierke's association-theory does map out a possible middle
course between the atomistic individualism which has grown from
a natural rights and social contract background and the organic
authoritarianism which has been the usual product of idealizations
of the state. Gierke himself tries always to maintain a balance
between free association, the embodiment of the *Genossenschaft*-
principle, and authority, the expression of the *Herrschaft*-principle.
By interposing free associations with their own spheres of right
between the state and the individual, Gierke attempts to provide
for the freest and most complete and effective expression of all
aspects of man's social nature, which is not, and can not be, entirely absorbed by the state. At the same time, through his insistence upon the organic nature of these associations, whose reality transcends the reality of the individual members, through
his conception of their organic integration in a hierarchy crowned
by the state, and in spite of his attempt to restrict the authority
of the state by the recognition of group-rights as well as those of
individuals, he leaves the way open for the practical subordination
of the lower by the higher and for the final sovereignty of the state.
Thus, while certain aspects of the *Genossenschaft*-principle are
principles of a liberty more positive than the liberty of individualism, its organic aspect also provides a structure with which his
authoritarian *Herrschaft*-principle is easily united.

It is apparent that the *Genossenschaft*-theory raised no question in Gierke's own mind about the validity of the accepted, conventional doctrine of state sovereignty. He does not present a
thoroughly convincing demonstration of the necessity in his system of the sovereign state, nor does he give any evidence that the
sovereignty he postulates is found in fact—partly at least for the

reason that such demonstrations would have appeared super-fluous to him.

To regard Gierke as a "pluralist" is obviously quite erroneous in view of the dominant role he assigns to the state and to state law. The pluralist elements of his theory are always carefully bal-anced by the organic and authoritarian. A loyal Prussian from the first, his devotion to Prussia and the monarchy, and his apprecia-tion of the advantages of assured unity tip the balance steadily towards authority. When unity and authority are challenged, his emphasis upon unity and stability comes to more forceful ex-pression, but the emphasis is one implicit always in his own inter-pretation of the *Genossenschaft*-theory.

Logically it might be argued that Gierke's original principles of association should lead to a federal structure which might easily include, as constituent members, functional as well as territorial units. And his interest in administrative reform in the direction of territorial decentralization seems to look in this direction. But here again state, monarchy, and Prussia stand in the way of com-plete and logical development of the *Genossenschaft*-principle.

CHAPTER IX

I have attempted to point out in detail the two antithetic tendencies which run through Gierke's development of the *Genossenschaft*-theory. The first, stressing the spontaneous unity of associated groups and their autonomous or semi-autonomous position in a social whole, is a tendency which ran counter to the temper of German academic thought in the nineteenth century, and which required, therefore, the support of the traditions of an earlier past. The second, stressing the organic integration of associated groups in a larger whole and the special position of the sovereign state and the monarchy, was, as Gierke himself realized, quite in the tradition of the German thought of his period.

I. The latter, traditional tendency was one which built upon the basis laid by Hegel, who first gave the organic theory "a statement which in its essence remained almost unchallenged in Germany throughout the nineteenth century and still commands the allegiance of the majority of political thinkers."[1] An appeal to the concepts of organic unity and of the real, organic personality of the state was the response of Hegel, as of less metaphysical thinkers,[2] to the atomizing individualism of eighteenth century rationalists. "Not only was the state not a contractual relationship between a number of individuals, but it was itself an Individuality, independent of and superior to all other individuals; a Person taking all other persons into itself and bringing to them that universality and fulness which otherwise they must lack.[3] Furthermore,

> the state is the realization of the ethical idea or ethical spirit. . . . The state, as the realization of substantive *will*, having its reality in the particular *self-consciousness* raised to the plane of the universal, is abso-

---

[1] Emerson, *op. cit.*, p. 13.
[2] *Cf.*, for England. Edmund Burke, *Reflections on the French Revolution*, in *Works*, World Classics edition, IV, p. 106.
[3] Emerson, *op. cit.*, p. 12.

lutely *rational*. This substantive unity is its own self-motivated, absolute end. . . . This end has the highest right over the individual whose
highest duty is to be a member of the state.[4]

The extremes to which this approach sometimes led Hegel himself are suggested in the well-known quotation:

> The state is the spirit which exists in the world and there consciously
> realizes itself. . . . It is the manifestation of God in the world, that
> is the state. . . . As the idea of state one must not hold before his eyes
> particular states . . . one must rather picture for himself the idea, this
> genuine God.[5]

The imposing list of writers included in van Krieken's critical
study of the organic theory[6] gives evidence of the hold of the
organic concept upon respectable post-Hegelian German theorists.
And Gierke's rather bitter attack upon van Krieken in defense
of "the greatest achievements of modern German public-law
theory"[7] gives evidence of Gierke's thorough acceptance of the
dominant theory. Erich Kaufmann, after tracing the organic concept of the state from Hegel through Stahl, Gerber, Held, con-
cludes that it was Gierke's greatest theoretical achievement to have
introduced the organic concept into the *juristic* construction of the
state.[8]

Emerson points out that the field of German juristic theory of
recent years has been divided between the Neo-Kantians whose
emphasis upon form and methodology brings them close to the
older formalists best represented by Laband, and the Neo-Hegel-
ians who continue the tradition of the organic approach. To me it
seems a most significant coincidence that the most uncompromising
of the Hegelians, Erich Kaufmann, was once a student of Gierke
and professes to be a follower of Gierke.[9] Not only this, but he
also claims to teach the true interpretation of his master in distinc-

---

[4] Hegel, *Philosophie des Rechts*, in *Werke* (ed. Gans, 3rd ed., 1854), VIII, secs. 257-258.

[5] *Ibid.*, sec. 258.

[6] Albert Th. van Krieken, *Über die sogenannte organische Staatstheorie: ein Beitrag zur Geschichte des Staatsbegriffs* (1873). For comment upon the influence, particularly through Lieber, Bluntschli, and Burgess, upon American writers, see, among others Kaufmann, *Auswärtige Gewalt und Kolonialgewalt in den Vereinigten Staaten von Amerika*, in *Staats- und völkerrechtliche Abhandlungen*, VII, No. 1 (1908). See also Merriam, *History of the Theory of Sovereignty since Rousseau* (1900) and Coker, *Organismic Theories of the State* (1910).

[7] "Die Grundbegriffe des Staatsrechts . . . ," p. 301.

[8] Kaufmann, *Über den Begriff des Organismus in der Staatslehre des 19 Jahrhunderts* (1908), p. 32.

[9] *Cf. ibid.*

tion from the misinterpretation widely publicized by Hugo Preuss. In a brief summary of Hegel's philosophy of the state, Kaufmann describes Hegel's concept of the state as follows:

> This genuine dialectic of civil society penetrates particularly to the state as the realization of the moral idea. In it the striving of individual, family, and civil society for perfection and unity finds its final fulfillment. As final unity and original moral idea, it branches out and differentiates itself in civil society, family, individual. . . . The state is a moral organism. It is the nature of an organism that, when one member assumes an independent position, all must go to ruin; that the law of the whole dwells in all members.[10]

In his development of Hegel's principles, Kaufmann sometimes reaches conclusions which are, to say the least, startling to an American mind. The distinguishing feature of the state is *Macht* —*Macht* clothed with moral purpose, to be sure, but still *Macht*. "The essence of the State is the development of power, is the will to assert itself and make itself effective in world history."[11] "War is the highest achievement of the State, bringing its genius to the finest flower. Peace, on the contrary, he [Kaufmann] described as a concept without any positive meaning, having significance only when put beside its counterpart, war: 'It has meaning only as a term for the end of a struggle for goods.' "[12] As a principle of international law should be recognized the maxim: "nur der, der kann, darf auch."[13]

And yet Kaufmann claims to be a follower of Gierke. How is that possible? The explanation is simple. Kaufmann develops one of Gierke's two conflicting tendencies, organic authoritarianism, to the point where it eclipses entirely the other. He exaggerates the authoritarian element until his own interpretation of Gierke becomes almost identical with his uncompromising interpretation of Hegel.

Among the jurists of the last generation, Adolf Lasson, it seems, would qualify for the position now held by Kaufmann, with the difference, however, that Lasson apparently was not influenced

---

[10] "Hegels Rechtsphilosophie," lecture in *Hegel-Feier der . . . Universität zu Berlin . . .* (1932), pp. 23-24.
[11] Kaufmann, *Das Wesen des Völkerrechts und die Clausula rebus sic stantibus* (1911), p. 135. cited in Emerson, *op. cit.,* p. 190.
[12] Emerson, *op. cit.,* p. 191, paraphrasing and quoting Kaufmann, *Das Wesen des Völkerrechts . . .* , pp. 151-152.
[13] Kaufmann, *Das Wesen des Völkerrechts . . .* , p. 152, cited in Emerson, *op. cit.,* p. 191, n. 63.

by Gierke. The Hegelian flavor of the following quotation is patent:

> The State is the highest and last of all natural things, as the law which is the content of its will is the highest and last of all natural systems. The empirical individual is for the activity of the State nothing but an object serving the State's end. . . . He is used with his strength for the ends of the State, and, if necessary, consumed. . . . Hence the natural individual with his interests is sacrificed for the State as soon as it is necessary.[14]

Even the moderate Josef Kohler, for whom the state is an "organic unit of the highest order," the function of which is to protect and develop human culture, comes in the end very close to Kaufmann's extreme Hegelianism. For the state

> everything and everybody is to be sacrificed. Here are no higher interests to which the existence of the State might be subordinated, here there does not even exist the possibility, which exists for the private citizen, of the State's sacrificing itself in spite of its right of self-defense and renouncing that right. Because for the State existence is not only a right, but a sacred duty: the unconditioned duty of self-preservation holds for the State since in the State is contained a great fullness of cultural forces the preservation of which is entrusted to it.[15]

In addition to these Hegelian or Neo-Hegelian jurists, for whom the organic state becomes scarcely distinguished from the *Machtstaat*, we find among contemporary German theorists numerous writers who, belonging to no general school of thought, still reach conclusions not far removed from the conclusions of the Hegelians. Of these, Carl Schmitt and Othmar Spann have enjoyed immense popularity among young university students during very recent years. If one may judge by the extreme popularity of their books, their immediate influence, academically and politically, must be worthy of notice.

To Carl Schmitt the state is "an over-individual phenomenon" whose authority is not derived from individuals, but is original.[16] It exists for the realization of law, and it alone has an obligation to law. The individual, in turn, exists simply for carrying out the will of the state. Thus the state stands as an intermediary agency

---

[14] Lasson, *System der Rechtsphilosophie* (1882), pp. 289-290, quoted in Emerson, *op. cit.*, p. 188.
[15] *Not kennt kein Gebot* (1915), p. 33; cited in Emerson, *op. cit.*, pp. 197-198.
[16] *Der Wert des Staates und die Bedeutung des Einzelnen* (1914), p. 85.

between law and the individual, and the subjugation of the individual to the state is, ultimately, subjugation to law.[17]

> So the state is not an instrument which men have made for themselves; on the contrary, it makes an instrument of every individual. The great super-personal organization is not fashioned by individuals as their creation; it does not fall within the sphere of means and purposes of so and so many individuals. . . .[18]
>
> . For the state, the individual as such is the accidental bearer of its only natural task, of the definite function it has to fulfill.[19]
>
> Whatever value may be attributed to individual men arises from submission to the over-individual rhythm of legality.[20]
>
> The individual has significance only in so far as he is an official of the state. . . . (*Der Einzelne nur so viel bedeutet, als er Beamte ist.* . . .)[21]

In Schmitt's system, then, the individual *qua* individual is completely irrelevant. The individual requires consideration only when and in so far as the state acts through him. To the objection that his theory must lead to paralyzing bureaucracy, Schmitt replies that such a charge can only arise from a misunderstanding of his theory which confuses the state with what is understood in *Tagespolitik* as "the government," and "since this discussion is not about political affairs,"[22] the objection is irrelevant. Although not entirely relevant here, it is perhaps of some significance that one of the most popular of Schmitt's books is *The Dictatorship,* a scholarly historical and logical study of the concept of the dictatorship.[23] Following this study, Schmitt published a study of modern parliamentarism in which he pointed out the present difficulties of liberal parliamentary democracy and the tendency of democracy towards dictatorship.[24]

Othmar Spann, in all of his writings, attacks bitterly every shade of individualism. Like the Italian Fascist, Rocco, he throws even Marxian Socialism into the group of mechanical and individualistic theories which he condemns. The theory which he presents in opposition to all individualistic approaches he labels "universalism." The essence of this "universalism" would seem to be the

---

[17] *Ibid.*, pp. 85-93, 52-53.
[18] *Ibid.*, p. 93.
[19] *Ibid.*, p. 86.
[20] *Ibid.*, p. 93.
[21] *Ibid.*, p. 91.
[22] *Ibid.*, p. 53.
[23] *Die Diktatur. von den Anfängen des modernen Souveränitätsgedankens bis zum proletarischen Klassenkampf* (1921).
[24] *Die geistesgeschichtliche Lage des heutigen Parlamentarismus* (1926).

organic integration of all individuals into a hierarchy of estates or classes (*Stände*).[25] This structure, he explains, would be a decentralized structure—but notice the peculiar meaning of his "decentralization."

> Decentralization means, further, that *authority in regard to the estates will proceed not up from below, but down from above.* The lower estate *does not delegate* to the higher power its right to rule, as in a democracy, but it *receives* from the higher unity its right, its position, and its articulation. . . .[26]

In this system, the state is but one of the "estates" (*Stände*), but it is not built upon other estates by integration or federation, nor, of course, from individuals. It must have its own independent source.

> The estates stand formally under the leadership of the state, because the state, as the highest estate, is the only one in a position and [therefore] delegated to present a collective unity in the domain of action. On the other hand, the state does not derive its power to rule from the other estates, and still less from single individuals. . . . *The state originates in itself*; it rests neither upon a professional "economic parliament" nor upon a "parliament" which "represents the whole people"; it rests, like every other estate, upon its own circle of human beings who devote themselves to its particular function and are its bearers.[27]

The state would seem to be, then, rulers who are able to rule! This ruling aristocracy is not to be chosen "by the majority from below," but takes its place by virtue of its ability to rule and lead.[28] And the leaders best demonstrate their leadership by their "militant spirit" and by "warfare." "The spirit of the true statesman, like that of the state-forming and state-bearing estate, is based upon *his own training for leadership* through the militant spirit and warfare rather than mere office-holding. . . ."[29]

Enough has been said, I believe, to demonstrate the importance of the organic approach in contemporary German theory. The organic concept, in some form or other, still dominates much of German thought;[30] and it leads frequently to amazing conclusions

---

[25] Cf. *Der wahre Staat* (1922), 1931 ed., pp. 151-152.
[26] *Ibid.*, p. 193.
[27] *Hauptpunkte der universalistischen Staatsauffassung* (1929), p. 8.
[28] *Der wahre Staat*, p 226.
[29] *Ibid.*, p. 257.
[30] I do not quite see the basis for Professor Coker's general statement that "the organic conception of political society' . . . has no longer, in either its pseudo-biologic or its more metaphysical form, any significant place in political theory." F. W. Coker, *Recent Political Thought* (1934), p. 26, n. 27.

which perhaps would not be quite so amazing to one raised in the atmosphere of Prussian politics and scholarship. I have omitted from the discussion above mention of such writers as Moeller van den Bruck whose book on *The Third Reich* (*Das dritte Reich*), written, so far as I know, with no reference whatever to the National-Socialist movement, undoubtedly trained many university students for the ranks of the "S.A." Still it should be obvious that the doctrines of National-Socialism were sown on not unfertile ground. Such, then, is the result of the unbalanced development of one side—the traditional German side—of Gierke's theory.

I have pointed out repeatedly that the authoritarian element in Gierke's theory is strengthened by his acceptance of the institution of monarchy and his devotion to the Prussian monarchy. Gierke, of course, was not alone in this devotion. The strong hold of monarchic concepts upon the writers of Gierke's period and the consequent importance of monarchic *Obrigkeit* (authority) in their theories is scarcely in need of demonstration. Conrad Bornhak, a contemporary of Gierke, expresses a common view when he says:

> The German States rested from the time of absolute monarchy on the monarchical principle according to which all the rights of political power are united in the person of the monarch and every right and every duty of the State refers back to the physical person of the monarch. The transition to the constitutional system altered nothing of this. The constitutions found their legal basis in the legislative right of the monarch who until then was absolute. He did not govern on the strength of the constitution, even if restricted to its limits, but the constitution existed on the strength of his will.[31]

In 1908 Kaufmann can still say:

> The official and ruling theory of the state of the nineteenth century was truly the *state theory of the monarchic principle.* . . . It attributed *state* sovereignty entirely to the person of the princely ruler, and construed the constitution not as a basic law coming from the state-whole, but as a voluntary limitation of a monarch sovereign in his own right. . . . And we shall be obliged to admit, further, that the theory of the monarchic principle is not to be considered dead even today.[32]

---

[31] Conrad Bornhak, *Grundriss des deutschen Staatsrechts* (5th ed., 1920) cited in Emerson, *op. cit.*, p. 213.
[32] *Auswärtige Gewalt* . . . , p. 192.

The hold of the monarchy, popularly as well as academically, is well expressed by Friedrich Meinecke on the eve of the World War:

> We will allow no disturbance of the national monarchy, in which we recognize the foundation and cornerstone of our state life. Its value to us is not merely rational; it has an irreplaceable emotional value. However bravely the German dares to fly into the realm of ideas, still his heart opens wide only when a living personality appears before him as the bearer of the idea. We are not satisfied with the consciousness that our nation is a great spiritual collective personality, but we demand for it a leader for whom we can go through fire. Since the days of the Romans who first described us, no characteristic of the Germans has remained so firmly fixed as the 'need for personal loyalty.[33]

"The spirit of the Prussian people is monarchical through and through, *Gott sei dank*!"[34] The evidence would suggest that this remark of Bismarck was as true of the whole German people up until the Revolution as of the Prussian people in the Chancellor's day.[35] The monarchies were destroyed by the Revolution. Whether the principle of *Obrigkeit* was so completely destroyed as the institution with which it was so closely associated is another question, concerning which our answer today can scarcely be so confident as it might have been a decade ago.

II.   When we turn to the second tendency implicit in Gierke's theory, we may safely say, I believe, that Gierke's influence here was probably greater outside Germany than within. It may have been purely accidental that in the year 1933 no one of the large public or university libraries in Berlin owned a copy of Maitland's translation of Gierke. But the fact may also have more than symbolic significance. Certainly it is true that, in developing the *genossenschaftlich* side of his theory Gierke had to struggle against the weight of academic tradition not only from without, but even from within himself.

The single important German theorist to develop the *genossenschaftlich* side of Gierke's theory was Hugo Preuss, a student

---

[33] Friedrich Meinecke, in *Logos*, IV (1913), pp. 171-172.
[34] *Otto von Bismarck—Deutscher Staat*, Bismarck documents ed. by Hans Rothfels (1925), p. 209, cited in Emerson, *op. cit.*, p. 75.
[35] For further evidence, see Emerson, *op. cit.*, pp. 73-77, 105, 124-125, 235-236. Emerson points out that adherence to the monarchic principle complicated the problem of construing the old *Reich*, since it made impossible the simple solution of lodging sovereignty with the people. Laband, for example, was forced to maintain that the *Reich* was not a juristic person of millions of members, but one of twenty-five members. *Cf.* Emerson, *op. cit.*, p. 105. For Gierke's recognition of this point see p. 83, *supra*.

of Gierke whose interpretation of the *Genossenschaft*-theory led him to a position almost diametrically opposite that of Gierke's other well-known student, Kaufmann.[36]

In his early writings, Preuss was interested primarily in administrative reforms which would transform the authoritarian German state dominated by Prussia into a decentralized, unitary democratic state. The federalism of the old *Reich* he regarded as a sham which hid the real dominance of Prussia. The proper path towards a transformation led through Gierke's *Genossenschaft*-theory. *Gemeinde,* member-state, and *Reich* must be recognized as organic persons homogeneous with each other. "Designating the state as organism and as person does not differentiate it from all other collective units; on the contrary, it emphasizes its similarity."[37] "Not the theoretical antithesis, but the theoretical homogeneity of *Gemeinde* and state as associational collective-persons is the basic idea of the reform."[38]

But Preuss pushed this *Genossenschaft* conception far beyond the point Gierke was willing to permit. Gierke had clung to the concept of state sovereignty; Preuss discards sovereignty—that "spider's web" which only entangles political theory.[39] "The feudal tie was the ideal basis of the feudal state; *for the construction of the legal state (Rechtsstaat) there is required a third principle, specifically different. . . .* In short, it must be decided finally to strike the concept of sovereignty out of the *dogma* of our political theory, and to consider it only an historic concept similar to the feudal principle."[40] Preuss does not attempt to minimize this divergence from his master's system, but he does point out that Gierke's system was developed primarily for private law and can not, therefore, be applied to public-law problems entirely without change. He then remarks, "Never do I feel myself more thoroughly Gierke's follower than when I disagree with him."[41]

Preuss' abandonment in 1918-1919 of his earlier stand is a matter of common knowledge. As a result of the war, Prussian

---

[36] In conversation with the writer, Professor Kaufmann has stated that Gierke prepared *Das Wesen der menschlichen Verbände* for the purpose of correcting misinterpretations of his theory which were being publicized particularly by Preuss.

[37] *Gemeinde, Staat, Reich* (1889), p. 175.

[38] "Die Lehre Gierkes und das Problem der preussischen Verwaltungsreform," in *Festgabe der Berliner juristischen Fakultät für Otto Gierke zum Doktor-Jubilaum, 21 Aug., 1910* (1910), p. 261.

[39] *Gemeinde, Staat, Reich,* p. vi.

[40] *Ibid.,* pp. 93-94.

[41] *Ibid.,* p. vii.

control and the *"Obrigkeit*-system" were destroyed. Or, more accurately, as Preuss points out, they simply collapsed—since their destruction was not caused from within by a revolutionary group. Here, then, was a possible opportunity to realize the decentralized *Volksstaat* which Preuss had so long demanded. But with national unity threatened, on the one hand, by the possibility of secession, and, on the other, by the radical demands of those who advocated a soviet or council system, Preuss was forced to throw his weight on the side of national unity and centralization.

> A union of twenty-five "sovereign" peoples would have been the death of the national state. The basis of the constitutional structure of the democratic republic could be only the national unity of the German people. . . . That the unity of people and *Reich* is the primary consideration, division into *Länder* only secondary . . . is the leading principle which permeates the whole content of the constitution of Weimar.[42]

Was the system established by the Weimar Constitution *Bundesstaat* or unitary state? What, after all, is the theoretical distinction? On this pedants' problem a whole library has already been written, says Preuss; but still no satisfactory distinction has been found between the member-state of the *Bundesstaat* and the autonomous province of the unitary state. The truth is that "even the keenness of German scholarship can find nothing where there is nothing to be found."[43] Speaking practically in answer to the Bavarian claims, Preuss insists that "the German Republic is by no means a union of single states, but simply *the German state*; the *Länder* are subdivisions of the united German state-people, which submit to transformation according to the vital interests of the national state."[44]

Thus the one follower of Gierke who, stressing decentralization and federalism, was led even to denial of state sovereignty in his early career, was forced in the end into uncompromising affirmation of the united, centralized, and sovereign state. Specific, practical problems forced Preuss toward conclusions similar to those which Gierke, conditioned by his background and temperament, naturally sought.

---

[42] *Deutschlands republikanische Reichsverfassung* (1920), pp. 12-13.
[43] *Ibid.*, p. 9.
[44] *Der deutsche Nationalstaat* (1924), p. 137; *cf.* also *Um die Reichsverfassung von Weimar* (1924); *Reich und Länder* (1928).

Brief mention might be made of the pluralistic views of Walter Rathenau. Rathenau shows no evidence of any knowledge of Gierke—nor of any academic theories. He was an industrialist, who, brought into contact with political problems by his service on a war-time supply board, took an active part in post-revolutionary politics until his assassination in 1922. Rathenau was impressed by the complicated network of associations—civil, territorial, professional, social, spiritual, religious—which bind all individuals, some of them leading to the political state as a center, many of them seemingly quite independent of the state.[45] Within the political, juridical state Rathenau saw the growth of the military, the religious, the administrative, the educational, the commercial and the economic states. All of these states are even today practically autonomous, but subject in some of their decisions to the political state.[46] The political state with its political parliament is inadequate to deal with this complicated pluralistic system. It should be replaced by a series of "functional states," built from below on the basis of interest or cultural groupings, and culminating in a functional parliament and functional ministry under the leadership of a political minister from the political parliament.[47] Rathenau's books and speeches[48] represent, I should say, the effort of a conservative, intelligent industrialist to envisage a new social organization which would avoid the necessity of "state-economy, forceful economy, and bureaucracy." In a sense, it is an answer to Communist advocates of the council-system (*Räte-system*), which would substitute rationalization and self-discipline for state control.

III. It is not my purpose here to compare the development by German writers of the two tendencies described with that of non-German writers. But, in order to indicate the difference in approach between Anglo-American "pluralists" and the writers mentioned above, I wish to conclude with a brief comparison between the ideas of Harold Laski, as the most important Anglo-American exponent of pluralism, and those of Gierke.

I think that it is safe to characterize Laski as an ethical individualist who, recognizing the undesirable consequences of ex-

---

[45] *Der neue Staat* (1919), pp. 11-12.
[46] *Ibid.*, p. 28.
[47] *Ibid.*, p. 38.
[48] *Cf.* also *Gesammelte Reden* (1924); *Von kommenden Dingen* (1922; translated under the title *In Days to Come* by E. and C. Paul); *Kritik der dreifachen Revolution.*

treme individualism as revealed, for example, in Rousseau's popular sovereignty and absolute majority rule,[49] attempts to avoid these consequences by emphasizing the complexity of men's will and interest, and hence, the impossibility of absorbing either by any single institution. "Authority must be based upon consent," he tells us repeatedly.[50] No authority can demand men's loyalty; every organization of men must win the loyalty of its members. And no association of men can absorb completely the loyalty of any individual. Associations of wider scope, including the state, must always be built upon the *non-absorptive* integration of individuals *and* of lesser associations. Laski is thus led to his vigorous defense of the spontaneous origin and intrinsic value of associations and, therefore, of their reality and rightful claim to a position of independence coordinate with that of the state.

> The State . . . does not exhaust the associative impulse in men. They build themselves groups as the expression of felt needs which can not be satisfied by individual activity. The group is an attempt to advance some interest in which its members feel an answer to the wants of their experience. . . . The group is real in the same sense as the State is real. It has, that is to say, an interest to promote, a function to serve The State does not call it into being. It is not, outside the categories of law, dependent upon the State. . . . The group is real, I suggest, as a relation or a process. It is a binding together of its individual parts to certain modes of behavior deemed by them likely to promote the interests with which they are concerned. In that sense it possesses personality. It results in integrated behavior. It enables its members to find channels of satisfied activity which, otherwise, would be absent. It has life only through that behavior. It lives, not as a thing apart from its members, but in and through what they do.[51]

Laski then goes on to demonstrate that the traditional concept of sovereignty is without past or present factual foundation, and is logically and ethically untenable.[52] Sovereignty being eliminated, the state becomes homogeneous with other associations, which, together with individuals, compose the state.

> Nothing is more stupid than for the state to regard the individual and itself as the only entities of which account must be taken, or to suggest

---

[49] *Cf.*, e.g., *Grammar of Politics*, pp. 29 ff.; *Foundations of Sovereignty*, pp. 213-214.
[50] *E.g.*, *Grammar of Politics*, pp. 29, 62.
[51] *Ibid.*, pp. 255-256.
[52] *Cf.*, e.g., *ibid.*, p. 271; *Authority in the Modern State*, p. 308. Three of Laski's early studies deal with the subject: *The Problem of Sovereignty* (1917); *Authority in the Modern State* (1919); *The Foundations of Sovereignty* (1921).

that other groups live by its good pleasure. That is to make the easy mistake of thinking that the activities of man in his relation to government exhaust his nature. It is a fatal error. . . .

For the state there are found subjects of social rights and duties. They are not the creation of the state; the state is simply an organization for the realization of an end. The subjects of those rights are sometimes individual human beings; sometimes they take the form of fellowships of men. These fellowships possess a personality into the nature of which it is not here necessary to examine. The fundamental fact for the state is that they present an activity that is unified and must be taken as involving the possession of rights.[53]

The state is only one among many forms of human associations. It is not necessarily any more in harmony with the end of society than a church or a trade-union or a free-masons' lodge.[54]

Upon this basis, political authority can only be decentralized and federalistic: federalistic not merely geographically but also functionally.

Because society is federal, authority must be federal also. . . . [This means, for example] making the mining industry a unit of administration in the same sense as Lancaster. It means surrounding the ministry of education with bodies entitled to speak on behalf of the parties to the educational process. . . .[55]

The mistake we have made in the past is to think of federal government in terms simply of area and distance. . . . We must learn to think differently. . . . There is a clear tendency on the part of industrial and professional groups to become self-governing. Legislation consecrates the solutions they evolve. They become sovereign in the sense—which, after all, is the only sense that matters—that the rules they draw up are recognized as the answer to the problems they have to meet. . . . What obviously must be done is to secure the limitation of [the state's] activities on the one hand, and the independence of its instruments on the other. But the functions so delimited demand, in return, their organization, and we are thus driven back to federal government.[56]

It is important to notice that Laski does not use the term "federalism" in a technical, juristic sense. His "federalism" would be just as possible in the decentralized unitary state as in a federal state.[57]

[53] *Authority in the Modern State*, pp. 56-57.
[54] *Ibid.*, p. 65.
[55] *Grammar of Politics*, p. 271.
[56] *Authority in the Modern State*, pp. 385-386.
[57] *Cf.* his excellent statement of the practical implications of his position in "The Problem of Administrative Areas," in *Smith College Studies in History*, IV (1918-1919), pp. 1 ff.

In spite of himself, Laski is frequently led into statements which bring him very close to the position of the Rousseau school, which he has rejected. For the state, whose legal sovereignty he finally recognizes as necessary,[58] is not simply a supreme authority endowed with the function of conciliating clashes between lesser associations, as the Gild Socialists would have it; but it has a distinct purpose of its own. It "controls the level at which men are to live as men"; its purpose is the fulfillment of the "general end" of society. "It is the association to protect the interests of men as citizens."[59]

Thus Laski's position differs from that of Preuss in its emphasis always upon the individual and its omission of the notion of organism. And from the position of Gierke it is even more widely separated by its complete repudiation of the tempering element of authority from above as well as by the absence of the organic concept. In Laski, as in others of the Anglo-American pluralist school, there is more of Rousseau and Proudhon than of Gierke.

---

[58] *Cf. Foundations of Sovereignty*, pp. 236-237; *Grammar of Politics*, pp. 69 ff.
[59] *Grammar of Politics*, p. 70.

BIBLIOGRAPHY

I. Works of Otto Von Gierke.

"Das alte und das neue deutsche Reich," in Fr. von Holtzendorff and W. Oncken, *Deutsche Zeit- und Streitfragen*, Vol. III, No. 35 (1874).

Das deutsche Genossenschaftsrecht. 4 vols. Berlin, 1868-1913.
> Vol. I. *Rechtsgeschichte der deutschen Genossenschaft.* 1868.
> Vol. II. *Geschichte des deutschen Körperschaftsbegriff.* 1873.
> Vol. III. *Der Staats- und Korporationslehre des Alterthums und des Mittelalters und ihre Aufnahme in Deutschland.* 1881.
> Vol. IV. *Die Staats- und Korporationslehre der Neuzeit.* 1913.

Das Wesen der menschlichen Verbände, inaugural address upon assuming *Rektorat* at the University of Berlin, 15 Oct., 1902. Leipzig, 1902.

"Der deutsche Volksgeist im Kriege," in *Der deutsche Krieg*, No. 46 (Stuttgart and Berlin, 1915).

Der Entwurf eines bürgerlichen Gesetzbuches und das deutsche Recht. Leipzig, 1889.
Revision of articles which appeared under the same general title in (Schmollers) *Jahrbuch für Gesetzgebung, Verwaltung und Volkswirtschaft*, XII (1888), XIII (1889).

Deutsches Privatrecht. 3 vols. Leipzig, 1895 ff. Vol. I.

Der germanische Staatsgedanke, in *Staat, Recht, und Volk*, No. 5 (Berlin, 1919).

Die Genossenschaftstheorie und das deutsche Rechtssprechung. Berlin, 1887.

"Die Grundbegriffe des Staatsrechts und die neuesten Staatsrechts-theorien," in *Zeitschrift für die gesammte Staatswissenschaft,*

XXX (1874), pp. 153-198, 265-335. Reprinted as a separate work, Tübingen, 1915.

Die historische Rechtsschule und die Germanisten, lecture delivered at the memorial celebration for the founder of the University of Berlin, King Friedrich Wilhelm III, 3 Aug., 1903. Berlin, 1903.

"Georg Beseler," in *Zeitschrift der Savigny-Stiftung für Rechtsgeschichte (Germanische Abteilung),* X (1889), pp. 1-24.

"German Constitutional Law in its Relation to the American Constitution," in *Harvard Law Review,* XXIII, No. 4 (Feb., 1910), pp. 273-290.

"Grundzüge des deutschen Privatrechts," in Holtzendorff, *Encyklopädie der Rechtswissenschaft,* Vol. I. 1904.

Johannes Althusius und die Entwicklung der naturrechtlichen Staatstheorien. 4th ed., Breslau, 1929.

"Krieg und Kultur," in *Deutsche Reden in schwerer Zeit,* No. 2 (Berlin, 1914).

"Labands Staatsrecht und die deutsche Rechtswissenschaft," in (Schmollers) *Jahrbuch für Gesetzgebung, Verwaltung und Volkswirtschaft,* VII (1883), pp. 1097-1195.

Naturrecht und deutsches Recht, inaugural address upon assuming *Rektorat* at the University of Breslau, 15 Oct., 1882. Frankfort a. M., 1883.

Political Theories of the Middle Age. Tr. with introduction by F. W. Maitland. Cambridge, 1900.
This is a section of *Das deutsche Genossenschaftsrecht* (Vol. III, pp. 502-644) entitled "Die publizistischen Lehren des Mittelalters."

"Recht und Sittlichkeit," in *Logos,* VI, 3 (1917), pp. 211-264.

Rudolf von Gneist, memorial address before the *Juristischen Gesellschaft zu Berlin,* 19 Oct., 1895. Berlin, 1896.

Die soziale Aufgabe des Privatrechts, speech before the *Juristischen Gesellschaft zu Wien,* 5 April, 1889. Berlin, 1889.

"Über die Geschichte des Majoritätsprinzips," in *Essays in Legal History Read before the International Congress of Historical Studies, London, 1913.* Ed. by Paul Vinogradoff. Oxford, 1913, pp. 312-335.
Reprinted in (Schmollers) *Jahrbuch für Gesetzgebung, Verwaltung und Volkswirtschaft,* XXXIX (1915), pp. 565-587.

(A complete bibliography of Gierke's works is to be found in an appendix to Professor Stutz' article, "Zur Erinnerung an Otto von Gierke," in *Zeitschrift der Savigny-Stiftung für Rechtsgeschichte (Germanische Abteilung),* Vol. 43 (1922), pp. xlv ff.

Sobei Mogi, in *Otto von Gierke, His Political Theory and Jurisprudence,* London, 1932, presents an identical bibliography, but without any acknowledgment or reference to Stutz' article.)

II. Works of Other Writers.

Below, Georg von. *Das ältere deutsche Städtewesen and Burgertum.* Leipzig, 1898.
Der deutsche Staat des Mittelalters. Leipzig, 1914.

Boehm, Max H. "Federalism," in *Encyclopedia of the Social Sciences.* Vol. VI.

Brie, Siegfried. *Der Bundesstaat: eine historisch-dogmatische Untersuchung.* Leipzig, 1874.

Bruck, Moeller van den. *Das dritte Reich.*

Coker, F. W. *Organismic Theories of the State,* in *Columbia Studies in History, Economics and Public Law.* Vol. 38. New York, 1910.
Recent Political Thought. New York, 1934.

Commons, J. R. *Legal Foundations of Capitalism.* New York, 1927.

Dewey, John. *The Public and Its Problems.* New York, 1927.

Emerson, Rupert. *State and Sovereignty in Modern Germany.* New Haven, 1928.

Follett, M.P. *Creative Experience.* New York, 1924.
The New State. New York, 1918.

Friedrich, C. J., ed. *Politica Methodice Digesta of Johannes Althusius*, in *Harvard Political Classics*. Vol. II. Cambridge, 1932.

Gurwitch, Georg. "Otto von Gierke als Rechtsphilosoph," in *Logos*, XI (1922-1923), pp. 86-132.

Hänel, A. *Studien zum deutschen Staatsrechte*, Vol. I. 1873.

Hegel, G.W.F. *Grundlinien der Philosophie des Rechts*, in *Werke*. Vol. VIII. 3rd ed., 1854.

Ihering, R. von. "Im juristischen Begriffshimmel," in *Scherz und Ernst in der Jurisprudenz*. 1885.

Jellinek, Georg. *Die Lehre von den Staatenverbindungen*. Wien, 1882.

Kaufmann, Erich. "Auswärtige Gewalt und Kolonialgewalt in den Vereinigten Staaten von Amerika," in *Staats- und völkerrechtliche Abhandlungen*, VII, 1 (1908).
Das Wesen des Völkerrechts und die Clausula rebus sic stantibus. 1911.
"Hegels Rechtsphilosophie," lecture in *Hegel-Feier der . . . Universität zu Berlin am 14 Nov., 1931*. Berlin, 1932.
Über den Begriff des Organismus in der Staatslehre des 19 Jahrhunderts. Heidelberg, 1908.

Kierulff. *Theorie des germanisches Civilrechts*. 1839.

Krabbe, H. *The Modern Idea of the State*. Tr. by Sabine and Shepard. New York, 1922.

Krieken, A. T. van. *Über die sogenannte organische Staatstheorie: ein Beitrag zur Geschichte des Staatsbegriffs*. Leipzig, 1873.

Laband, Paul. *Das Staatsrecht des deutschen Reiches*. Vol. III. Tübingen, 1882.

Laski, H. J. *Authority in the Modern State*. New Haven, 1919.
The Foundations of Sovereignty. London, 1921.
Grammar of Politics. London, 1925.
"The Problem of Administrative Areas," in *Smith College Studies in History*, IV (1918-1919), pp. 1 ff.
Studies in the Problem of Sovereignty. New Haven, 1917.

Maitland, F. W. Introduction to translation of Gierke, *Political Theories of the Middle Age*. Cambridge, 1900.
Collected Papers. Vol. III. Cambridge, 1911.

Merriam, C. E. *History of the Theory of Sovereignty since Rousseau*, in *Columbia Studies*. Vol. XII. New York, 1900.

Merriam, C. E., and H. E. Barnes. *Political Theories, Recent Times*. New York, 1924.

Mogi, Sobei. *Otto von Gierke, His Political Teaching and Jurisprudence*. London, 1932.
The Problem of Federalism. 2 vols. London, 1931.

Pollock, F. "Has the Common Law Received the Fiction Theory of Corporations?" in *Festschrift Otto Gierke zum siebzigsten Geburtstag*. Weimar, 1911.

Preuss, Hugo. *Der deutsche Nationalstaat*. Frankfort, 1924.
Deutschlands republikanische Reichsverfassung. Berlin, 1920.
"Die Lehre Gierkes und das Problem der preussischen Verwaltungsreform," in *Festgabe der Berliner Juristischen Fakultät für Otto Gierke zum Doktor-Jubilaum, 21 August, 1910*. Vol. I. Breslau, 1910.
Gemeinde, Staat, Reich. Berlin, 1889.
Obrigkeitsstaat und grossdeutscher Gedanke. Jena, 1915.
"Die Persönlichkeit des Staates, organisch und individualistisch betrachtet," in *Archiv für öffentliches Recht*, IV (1889), pp. 62 ff.
Reich und Länder. Berlin, 1928.
"Über Organpersönlichkeit," in (Schmollers) *Jahrbuch für Gesetzgebung, Verwaltung und Volkswirtschaft*, XXVI (1902), 2, pp. 103 ff.
Um die Reichsverfassung von Weimar. Berlin, 1924.

Rathenau, Walter. *Der neue Staat*. Berlin, 1919.
Gesammelte Reden. Berlin, 1924.
Kritik der dreifachen Revolution. Berlin, 1919.
Von kommenden Dingen. 1921.
Translated under the title, *In Days to Come*, by E. and C. Paul. London, 1921.

Schmitt, Carl. *Der Wert des Staates und die Bedeutung des Einzelnen.* Tübingen, 1914.
\'*Die- Diktatur von den Anfängen des modernen Souveränitätsgedankens bis zum proletarischen Klassenkampf.* München and Leipzig, 1921.
Die geistesgeschichtliche Lage des heutigen Parlamentarismus. München and Leipzig, 1923.
Hugo Preuss; sein Staatsbegriff und seine Stellung in der deutschen Staatslehre. Tübingen, 1930.

Schultze, Alfred. "Otto von Gierke als Dogmatiker des bürgerlichen Rechts," in (Iherings) *Jahrbücher für die Dogmatik des bürgerlichen Rechts,* 2nd series, XXXVII (1921).

Spann, Othmar. *Hauptpunkte der universalistischen Staatsauffassung.* Berlin, 1929.
Der wahre Staat. Jena, 1931.

Stutz, Ulrich. "Zur Erinnerung an Otto von Gierke," in *Zeitschrift der Savigny-Stiftung für Rechtsgeschichte (Germanische Abteilung)*, Vol. 43 (1922), pp. vii ff.

Wright, B. F. *American Interpretations of Natural Law; a Study in the History of Political Thought.* Cambridge, 1931.

APPENDICES

TRANSLATIONS FROM GIERKE

A. Introduction to Volume I of *Das deutsche Genossenschafts-recht,* including Gierke's division of periods for the history of the German *Genossenschaft.* (A general statement of Gierke's approach and a very generalized summary of the conclusions of Volume I.)

B. "The Idea of Federalism." (This is Chapter V of Part II of Gierke's *Johannes Althusius und die Entwicklung der natur-rechtlichen Staatstheorien.* It is one of the best examples of Gierke's remarkable ability to trace and make lucid the development of a complex set of ideas. In addition, it contains Gierke's interpretation of writers whose ideas have historic relevance for this study.)

C. *The Nature of Human Associations.* (This is Gierke's statement of the philosophic basis of his system.)

D. *The Basic Concepts of State Law and the Most Recent State-Law Theories.* (The section translated here is- a discussion of methodology, and also of the application of Gierke's theory to jurisprudence and political theory.)

APPENDIX A.

INTRODUCTION TO VOLUME I OF *Das Deutsche Genossenschaftsrecht*[1]

What man is, he owes to the association of man with man. The possibility of historical development was given us in the capacity to form associations which not only add to the strength of those living today but, above all, bind past generations with the future through a permanence outlasting the personality of single members.

As the forward march of world-history is inevitably realized, there appears in an unbroken ascending arch the noble structure of those organic associations which, in ever greater and more comprehensive circles, bring into tangible form and reality the interdependence of all human existence, unity in its multi-colored variations. From marriage, the highest of those associations which do not outlast their members, grow forth in abundant gradations families, races, tribes and clans, *Gemeinde,* states and leagues of states; and for this development one can imagine no other limit than when, some time in the distant future, the whole of mankind shall be drawn together into a single organized community, which shall visibly demonstrate that all are but members of one great whole.

But this development from apparently unconquerable variety to *unity* presents only one side of social progress. All spiritual life, all human endeavors would perforce perish if the idea of unity were alone and exclusively triumphant. With equal force and equal necessity, the opposing idea breaks its way: the idea of persistent multiplicity in every realized (*zusammenfassenden*) unity, the idea of the rights and independence of all the narrower unities converging in the higher unity, even those of single individuals—the idea of *liberty.*

---

[1] *Das deutsche Genossenschaftsrecht,* I, *Rechtsgeschichte der deutschen Genossenschaft* (1868), pp. 1-4.

The conflict of these two great principles determines one of the mightiest movements in history. Their reconciliation in a form suitable to the time, nationality, culture and all other concrete relationships is a people's good fortune; the one-sided development of one or the other, the unequal or improper division of their realms, is its misfortune. . . .

Of all peoples mentioned in history, none has been so deeply and strongly affected by the antithesis described, none is by its inmost nature so capable of developing both ideas and therefore eventually harmonizing them, as is the Germanic. It seems almost as if this people alone were designated to create states which are at the same time united and free; almost as if the Latin peoples had a share in the process only in so far as they had received, with the fraction of Germanic blood flowing in their veins, a fraction of the Germanic characteristics, or as they had borrowed institutions created by Germanic spirit.

Inferior to no other people in their bent towards universality and in their capacity for political organization, superior to most in their love of freedom, the Germans above all others have a gift through which they have invested the idea of freedom with a special significance and based the idea of unity on a solid foundation—this is the gift of organizing associations. To be sure, the peoples of antiquity and numerous non-German peoples of today recognize numerous graduated natural and voluntary unions (*Verbände*) between the highest generality and the individual. But their love for corporate life, their sense of family, *Gemeinde*, and tribe, their capacity and desire for free association are in no way comparable with that inexhaustible Germanic spirit of association, which knows how to secure for all narrower members of the state an original, independent life, and which yet has the further power to create out of the still uncontrolled elements of national strength, for the most general as for the most particular purposes of human existence, an incalculable wealth of associations which are not animated from above but act spontaneously.

These narrower communities and associations, which in relation to the universal association (*Allgemeinheit*) appear as particulars, but in relation to their members as universals, offer the only possibility of uniting a large and inclusive state-unity with active civil liberty, with self-government. Their absence is the chief reason why so many Latin peoples lack civil liberty, their presence the surest safeguard of English and American liberty. Our German nation has suffered longer and more deeply under the antithesis than its sister nations, although it has equally, or perhaps *because* it has developed even more thoroughly than they those basic German concepts which strive toward universality as well as individual freedom, uniting both by means of the association. One might briefly say that, where unity was lacking, the independence of the members celebrated a dreary triumph, while in the single states the freedom of *Gemeinde* and associations had sunk to a miserable illusion in the face of an over-developed state unity. But the vigorous progress of our own day demonstrates that the German people recognizes its twofold goal; and permits us to hope that the latest among the unified European states will be the most perfect. And that force which distinguished the Germanic peoples from the beginning of history and arose again victoriously out of every ominous change—the creative force of association—is more living and active in the German people of today than in any other people.

(GIERKE'S DIVISION OF PERIODS FOR THE HISTORY OF THE GERMAN GENOSSENSCHAFT.)[2]

I. The *first period* extends from the earliest historical records to the coronation of Charlemagne (800). Although conditions at the beginning and the end of this thousand-year period have little in common, the two points can be brought together inasmuch as, during the whole period, German legal consciousness (*Rechtsbewusstsein*) continued to be bound to a thoroughly *patriarchal* conception of all human association. Moreover, the principle of original *folk-freedom* is, at the end of this period, still at least theoretically the basis of public life, although the opposing principle of *Herrschaft* and of *service* has of course already become the exclusive source of creative institutions. For this reason, throughout the whole period the basic form of all association is the *free association* (*freie Genossenschaft*) of the *old law,* which is consistent with the patriarchal folk-freedom, and which, as a personal peace- and right-union resting upon a natural interdependence, places all rights in the organization. But, from the beginning, the free association is faced by the opposite form of

---

[2] *Ibid.*, I, pp. 8-11.

organization, in which one is the bond for all: the *authoritarian union* in patriarchal, personal form; and this, in its inevitable development, forces the *Genossenschaft* ever further into the background. The struggle between *Genossenschaft* and *Herrschaft* involves a struggle between the old principle of the personality of all associations and the new principle of their impersonality (*Dinglichkeit*). The *Genossenschaften* develop into impersonal *Gemeinde*, the authoritarian units into manorial units, and so, even by the end of this period, the patriarchal constitutional principle is about to yield to a patrimonial concept of law and state.

II. In the *second period,* which extends to 1200, *Herrschaft* has definitely triumphed over the *Genossenschaft,* and impersonality over personality. The *patrimonial* and *feudal* constitutional principle rules the life of the nation. A mighty hierarchy of lords and servants towers up in Church and Empire and reaches to heaven itself, but every relation of dominion or service has become impersonal and therefore patrimonial. Only in subordinate positions and particularly in regions shut off from the great movement of the time does the old free *Genossenschaft* retain its higher significance. But so powerful is the corporative idea in the German spirit that it penetrates into the authoritarian organizations themselves, and first remakes, then dissolves them. Thus there arises as a new form of union, characteristic for this second period, the *dependent* or *authoritarian Genossenschaft*, which develops its own collective law (*Gesamtrecht*) beside and below the lord as the representative of its original unity. But already at the end of the period there is arising a younger, mightier principle, which finally beats the feudal state into fragments. This is the principle of free union (*Einung*), which, instead of the old associations based merely upon natural foundations, produces voluntary (*gewillkürte*) associations, but in the towns unites voluntary associations with the natural basis, and thus produces at the same time the oldest *Gemeinde* and the oldest state on German territory.

III. In the *third period,* which ends with the Middle Ages, it is the principle of *free union* (*Einung*) which, while feudal state and hierarchy are steadily falling to pieces, creates, working from below, organizations in the form of *optional* (*gekorenen*) *associa-*

tions in all spheres. Associations and associational unions, federally united, penetrate into ever higher spheres. They prepare the way for the emancipation of personality from the soil and territory, without, on the other hand, destroying the independence which has been won for the law of real property; they lead to a separation of public and private law; they develop the concept of the ideal collective personality as state, *Gemeinde*, corporation; and they almost succeed in building a united German state from below by free association.—Almost, but not quite! For the association of this period does not have the strength to complete its work. Unable to break through the limitations of the class structure, which it only fashions more rigidly, unable, above all, to draw the peasant class into the movement, it finally begins to harden into a fixed form. Thus it is not able to withstand a new force working toward the leveling of classes, the amalgamation of city and country, and a larger and more concentrated state unity. This force is territorial sovereignty (*Landeshoheit*), which succeeds in transforming the manor into the territorial state and in elevating itself to the position of solitary bearer of the modern idea of the state.

IV. In the *fourth period*—to 1806—comes the definite victory of territorial sovereignty and of the principle of *authority* (*Obrigkeit*) developed from it with the aid of the received Roman Law. The authoritarian idea of the state is developed and with it the police- and guardian-state. The associational institution is transformed into a privileged corporation, which takes its place as a purely private-law institution, and, thereby, gives up its claim of being a participant in public law. Over against these corporations, which no longer appear as members of the totality but as privileged particularities which are not, however, willing to undertake duties corresponding to their privileges, a unitary state authority which can humble or break them becomes a necessity. The old freedom and autonomy are of course thereby destroyed. The state moves outside and above the people; that which desires public meaning can exist only as a state institution, as a division of the state; the *dependent private-law corporation*—the characteristic form of organization of the period—is not able to recall its vanished public significance. The absolute state and absolute individuality become the catchwords of the time. But with the dissolution of all old organizations, territorial sovereignty at the same time destroys the privileges and inequalities of public law, and sets forth in the concept of subjects the equality of all before the law, and finally, for the first time in history, the individual freedom of all. However little civil liberty may accompany this development, however shamelessly the old political freedom and right of Germans may be destroyed, still this transition is necessary to prepare the ground for the civil liberty of all, which, in our century, takes the place of class liberty.

V. We stand at the threshold of the *fifth period,* in which we await the conciliation of traditional opposing principles through the ideas of a general state citizenry and of the representative state. Little as we have seen of this period, we may say already that its characteristic creative principle is and will be *free association* in its modern form. Through this principle, the German *Genossenschaft* has awakened, after a long death-like slumber, to more vigorous life, and has come to perfection. No longer bound by any class restriction, no longer limited by any exclusiveness, unendingly malleable in form, equally adapted for the noblest and the most trifling, the most far-reaching and the narrowest purpose, enriched by many qualities of Roman law, but contemptuous of the narrow Roman moulds into which theory and practice are ever trying to force it,—it is the reborn ancient association-idea of German law which has brought forth an incalculable complex of new forms of organization and filled the old with a new content. It has had a share in the transforming of the German *Gemeinde* and the German state, which have accomplished their progress so far and will progress further only through a return to the associational basis and through a revival of their associational elements. It is the sole creator of a free form of association which comprehends and refashions every phase of public and private life, which, great as its influence has been in the past, will be greater still in the near and distant future.

APPENDIX B.

THE IDEA OF FEDERALISM[1]

Among all the original characteristics of the political system of *Althusius* none is perhaps so startling as the spirit of *federalism* which pervades it from head to foot. Although the structure of society as a whole with corporate members was a basic idea of the true medieval system, there is still the difference that what in the medieval period was constructed from the top down is here reconstructed, through the idea of the social compact, from the bottom up. But it is even more remarkable that this federal structure of *Althusius* appears in league with that same sharply defined and concentrated concept of sovereignty which above all else had dissolved the medieval doctrine of composite social bodies, and which henceforth remained the chief instrument of efforts toward centralization!

I. The true *medieval* system of thought proceeded from the whole and from unity, but conceded to each more restricted whole, even to the individual, its own life, a special purpose, and an independent worth in the harmoniously constructed organism of a world filled with the spirit of God. So there resulted the thoroughly federalistic structure of the social whole, in harmony with the medieval manner of life. Although the theory postulated the visible unity of mankind in Church and Empire, yet it not only proceeded everywhere, simply on account of the dualism of the two swords, from the idea of two united orders, but also narrowed that unity to such dimensions as the universal purpose of mankind demanded. The universal union therefore appears as neither absolute nor exclusive, but forms only the spire of a social structure independently organized as a whole. And this principle then repeats itself in numerous steps down to the narrowest local vocational and domestic unions. Everywhere in church and state the unitary collective bodies take their being from the living mem-

---

[1] *Johannes Althusius und die Entwicklung der naturrechtlichen Staatstheorien* (4th ed., 1929), Part II, Ch. V.

119

ber-bodies, each of which requires connection with the higher whole but at the same time creates for itself a whole endowed with a special purpose and further organized within itself according to the principle of unity which begets and governs multiplicity. Between the highest generality and the inalienable unity of the individual there is introduced a series of intermediary unities, each of which embraces and includes the narrower unities. The theories of the publicists strive to create a fixed scheme for this organization, whereby in regard to the Church they may follow the accepted hierarchical organization, but in treating of worldly unions they may, by broadening the Aristotelian categories of associations, succeed in creating a parallel structure.

The first far-reaching shock befell this federalistic structure from the side of Church thought, since this elevated the papal system to the point of complete absorption of the state by the church on the one side, and on the other, to a centralization within the church which was deadening to the independent life of the members. Here also, however, the definite destruction of the proud edifice of thought was accomplished by the ancient conception of the state, revived by political and juristic thought, under whose influence theory was driven inevitably to the doctrine of the state as an *exclusive organization*.

To be sure, the prevailing thought, in accepting this notion that the state was simply human society, made a great reservation. It restricted this universality of state-society to considerations of the present welfare of human life, and reserved to the church as the society of eternal life a higher or at least equal right. Still the way was already prepared in the fourteenth and fifteenth centuries for the later absorption of the church by the state. Among the medieval publicists was one who dared to draw up a system, consistently developed in every detail, in which the church is simply a state establishment, the church property state property, spiritual offices state appointments, the church government a part of the state government, and the sovereign church-society identical with the citizenry. This was *Marsiglio of Padua*. No one followed him all the way. But single consequences of the same thought were drawn by other opponents of the hierarchy even in the medieval period. And even here the ancient doctrine that sacred law is a part of public law began in this sense to come into use.

For the rest the general philosophical political theory borrowed from Aristotle the definition of the state as, in distinction from the preliminary steps represented by family and *Gemeinde,* the highest, most complete and self-sufficient society. Were this concept realized, however, there could always be but one state among the human member-associations of higher or lower order. But this consequence was avoided by a crude inconsistency. For if the philosophers rediscover, in the medieval city-commonwealth, the *"polis"* or *"civitas"* as defined by Aristotle, and place over this, by virtue of the idea of the unitary organic structure of mankind, the completing and restricting bonds of *"regnum"* and *"imperium,"* then they obviously take back their definition immediately, and calmly transform the superlative into a comparative, the absolute into a relative attribute. And when the jurists, on the other hand, declare with the *Corpus Juris* that the Empire alone is a true state, while they define the concepts of *"civitas," "populus,"* and *"regnum"* in a manner consistent with the understanding of these concepts as *"Gemeinde"* or "provinces," then obviously, in spite of their state theory, they also make use continually of the narrower communities. But, once recovered, the classical state theory had to realize itself more and more in its exclusiveness. Indeed, at this point begins the philosophic state theory—often without further consideration of the hypothesis—that there is but one political organization, above which there is no room at all for a world-state and under which there is room for *Gemeinde* only. In jurisprudence, however, beginning with *Bartolus,* there was elaborated in continually sharper form the distinction between communities without and with superiors, and the equating of the former with the *imperium,* and, while the differences between *civitas, regnum,* and *imperium* were reduced from levels in the organic articulation of mankind to simple differences in size, the concept of state was monopolized by the *"universitates superiorem non recognoscentes."*

Thus even before the end of the Middle Ages the concentration of the state-concept was completed and the characteristic of *external sovereignty* was set up as the essential and distinguishing feature of the state. The *imperium mundi* over the sovereign state, in so far as it was not generally denied, was now in theory, as long since in practice, dissolved into substanceless shadow, and,

122 UNIVERSITY OF WISCONSIN STUDIES

at all events, stripped of the character of a political power. Under the sovereign state there was simply no room for states within a state, and all narrower communities had to fall within the rubric of *Gemeinde* and corporations.

But with the concentration of political life at one point, there was by no means a demand for the concentration of all associational life at this point. The medieval idea of the organic articulation of mankind was able to maintain itself in curtailed form within the sovereign state as the idea of the organic articulation of a people. To a certain degree, this was indeed the situation. The corporation-theory developed by jurisprudence upon the basis of Roman and canon law, and perfected to the finest detail, under which exclusively the narrow unions now fell, had indeed changed and destroyed from the ground up the Germanic concept of autonomous associational communities; nevertheless it had taken over enough of the content of this theory to preserve to all non-sovereign communities, as opposed to the avowedly exclusively sovereign state, an original and independent associational life, a sphere of public rights growing out of itself, an organic intermediate position between the individual and the highest generality. And within the political theory there was no lack, during the last centuries of the Middle Ages, so full of vigorous corporate life, of attempts to find a theoretical basis for the idea of corporative structure as opposed to the centralization in church and state—complete here, threatening there,— and to demonstrate in principle the independent value and the original right of the intermediate community.

Nevertheless, even in the Middle Ages the movement of theory that, on the whole, was not to be checked was in the direction of the exclusive sovereignty of the state to the point where the state would be the *exclusive representative of all social life*. As the content of the codified late-Roman law continually broke through all medieval-Germanic interpretations, jurisprudence was necessarily forced to a reinterpretation of the corporation theory in terms of a doctrine of association, which, while slow, was always in advance of actual changes in life. For this new theory, the state was the only source and the only subject of public law; the corporation, on the other hand, appeared merely as a delegated political creature in regard to the public sphere of rights accredited to it by the publicists, and in the realm of private law received the standing of an original subject of rights in the same degree as an individual only through the fictitious personality loaned it by the state. But the philosophical state theory, the more decidedly it stuffed itself with classical thought on the one hand, and, on the other, concealed in the individualistic natural-law doctrine all, that it had saved and developed of the opposing Christian-Germanic ideology of freedom, the more thoroughly prepared the way for the battle which filled the following centuries: in which the sovereign state and the sovereign individual wrangled over the boundaries of the spheres of their natural rights, and, in contrast, all intermediate communities were first degraded to mere more or less arbitrary creatures of positive law and finally were, in general, eliminated.

II. All these theoretical weapons of centralistic and atomistic tendencies forged in the Middle Ages grew stronger and broader *after the sixteenth century.*

Here let us consider briefly the extraordinary significance which the colossal change wrought by the Reformation in the relation of *church* and *state* had in this respect. As the church was more and more transformed from a rival for sovereignty into an institution of the state, the last great obstacle in the way of elevating the state to the position of an exclusive human organization disappeared. If the Reformers wished to maintain the conception of universal church unity in their concept of an invisible church, this was no legal concept. If they wished to continue the doctrine of *potestates distinctae,* neither in the Reformed constitutional ideal of a republican community identified with the congregation of the faithful nor in the Lutheran interpretation of the national character of the church through the episcopal system and the doctrine of three estates, did the separation of the *"regimen ecclesiasticum et saeculare"* mean more than a division of the administrative organization of one body. Finally, if the general medieval teaching was to be renewed from the side of Catholic doctrine, the general course of development of the ideas was not to be turned aside thereby, even in the Catholic world. And at last the pure territorial system, in which the complete absorption of the church by the state was theoretically accomplished, was victorious all along the line.

With the crumbling of the theory of a universal *Church* limiting the sovereignty of states, all that was perhaps still alive of the theory of a universal *Empire* limiting the sovereignty of states dwindled away also. Only as a lifeless phantom could the imperial publicists drag out the existence of the *imperium mundi*. In exchange for it, the medieval thought received in the natural-law theory a new form, full of life, in which, without detracting from the sovereignty of the single states, it undertook to deduce a bond of international law existing among them from a permanent and indestructible union. For since the sixteenth century the binding force of the *jus gentium* had been more and more often based upon a natural-law *"societas gentium,"* wherein the original and indestructible unity of mankind received proper expression, while at the same time full sovereignty was still preserved for each people. At all events, the idea of a company of states tended continually to pass over to the idea of the world state, which was then constructed, in opposition to the medieval world-monarchy, as a world-republic. But the prevailing theory expressly guarded itself against the assumption that the association of peoples gave the collectivity any power at all over the members, and admitted for the states, which in relation to each other remained in a state of nature, only natural obligations of a social sort similar to those of individuals before the founding of a state. The more forceful adherents of the doctrine of sovereignty in every century, however, chose to know about as little of the doctrine of a natural community of states as of the old doctrine of the positive-law authority of the world-state; or else they simply contested the legal nature of international law.

As against the churchly and international-law community, so in relation to narrower *unions of states* the doctrine of sovereignty was without exception developed by theory to the point where every possibility of a state over states was excluded. When federal structures, (or unions) were encountered in life, it was believed that one had only the choice between assuming an alliance (relations of union) among several fully-sovereign states, and assuming a decentralized unitary state. For this reason it was declared, on the one hand, that the formally organized federal structures and particularly the Swiss sworn association (*Eidgenossenschaft*) and the United Netherlands were simply alliances, in whose behalf one of course imported into the established doctrine of *foedera,* beside the several categories of equal and unequal alliances, the concept, more or less clearly distinguished from them, of the confederation erected through a *"foedus arctissimum"* and organized as *"Corpus confoederatum"* or *"Systema civitatum,"* yet with the fact brought always into sharpest relief, that even so close a union left the sovereignty of the single states unimpaired, that therefore they and they only were states, and that the whole bore, at the most, only the appearance of a state. On the other hand, the opposite concept of the unitary state was universally maintained, wherever one could not or did not care to attack the state-like nature of the whole; and this view was generally applied, but in particular to the German Empire.

Therefore, for the question of centralized or federal construction of the state, everything depended upon the question of whether and to what extent an original and independent social (*gemein*) life for the member-associations (*Gliedverbände*) remained consistent, within the unitary state, with the exclusive sovereignty of the whole which, through this sovereignty, was characterized as "state." It was in this setting, indeed, that *Althusius* constructed his federal system, since on this question he moved against the prevailing tendency just as definitely as he supported the strongest formulation of the doctrine of sovereignty in relation to the identification of state and church, the denial of a universal world union, and the rejection of a state constructed out of states.

The continuation by *jurisprudence* of the medieval *corporation theory* had the most decisive influence on the theoretical conception of the relation between the state and more restricted associations. The jurisprudence of the sixteenth century frequently entered the lists in behalf of the rights of *Gemeinde* and corporations, which were threatened by the increasingly powerful authoritarian state, and thereby in a significant sphere it upheld the idea of an original and independent public-law (*publicistischen*) domain for each *"universitas."* But on the whole all the rest of the conception of the corporation as a community was engulfed by the notion developed from Roman sources, that the legal subjectivity of the *universitas per se* means simply that it has a fictitious personality for private-law purposes, and that only in a special case, on the basis of special privilege, can it be endowed with certain public-law powers derived from the exclusive state law. Therefore the champions of corporative independence saw themselves ever more hard-pressed on these grounds, and sought only, on the one hand, to deduce from the private-law right of the *universitas* to its competence, a possible far-reaching circle of autonomous, self-governing rights based on itself; and, on the other hand, to protect the privileges stretching beyond this from withdrawal as *jura quaesita*. But while they fought so hard for the private-law conception of public-law (*publicistischer*) relations and for the maintenance of more extensive privileges, their absolutistic opponents met them from the beginning at the most obvious disadvantage, since the opponents could lead into the field in the battle for corporative independence the ideas of public law and of a common welfare (*Gemeinwohl*) taking precedence over privilege.

It is easy to understand that the modern absolutistic interpretation of the corporation theory found its inception in these tendencies in general political and *natural-law* theories pursued by the jurists. But here entered two more factors which worked to strengthen the tendency theoretically. At one time only the family regularly received the place of a necessary intermediary member between individual and state in the natural structure of society elaborated according to classical design; the *Gemeinde* was, at the best, recognized as the natural preliminary to the state which, therefore, completely disappeared as a natural-law organization in the complete state and reappeared only as a pure positive-law conception, together with corporations formerly regarded simply from the point of view of positive law. And so the doctrine of sovereignty drove forward until the conception of state power approached a conception of absorptive omnipotence, so that the power of other associations could be represented only as an overflow from the state. In both cases, *Bodin* above all developed the consequences of the principle with his careful and detailed handling of the "*collegia, corpora,* and *universitates*," and therefore thoroughly developed in regard to all narrower associations the conception of state institutions, although he differed greatly from al-

most all later absolutists in emphasizing their high political value
and the significance of an effective freedom for *Gemeinde* and
corporation. Among his followers, *Gregorius* practically surpassed
him on almost the same basis, and *Arnisaeus* and *Bornitz* would
recognize in *Gemeinde* and corporations nothing more than state
divisions for administrative purposes. The true proponents of
natural law developed very similar conceptions in so far as they
considered mention of *Gemeinde* and corporations at all worth the
trouble. Therefore, in the mass of textbooks and handbooks on
politics turned out since the beginning of the seventeenth century,
not only did the construction of all narrower associations as mere
state-institutions prevail more and more completely, but the narrower associations were also treated preponderantly from what
was simply a police point of view, in a spirit always inimical to
their freedom and independence. At the same time, the influence
of this natural-law and political conception was affecting more
and more decisively the positive doctrines of state law.

From this general tendency of development the *doctrine of
popular sovereignty* of the sixteenth century remained aloof, inasmuch as a strongly centralized state structure agreed as well
with its fundamental tenets as would a purely federalistic structure, and therefore neither in one direction nor in the other were
theoretical points of view of a particular sort developed from it.
But, in regard to practical applications, while among the Catholic
friends of the doctrine the centralized concepts predominated,
with a few Reformed "Monarchomachs" the idea of federalism
definitely broke through—in obvious connection with the federal
character of their church constitution derived from the *Gemeinde*
principle. It was *Languet* above all who considered single provinces and cities as guardians of the contract with God as well as
of the contract with the people, and, renewing the medieval theory,
claimed for them the right and duty of armed resistance against a
contract-breaking state power, and, in the last extreme, even the
right of breaking loose from the state.

It was *Althusius* again whose creative spirit fashioned into a
system and grounded upon a theoretical principle the federalistic
ideas which were fermenting in the movements of life and in the
views of his churchly and political circle. He accomplished this
simply by ruthlessly interpreting the concept of a social contract,

which he was the first to elevate into a principle, in its fundamental form as dissolving all public law into private law. So there resulted for him a pure natural-law social structure in which family, vocational association, *Gemeinde,* and province stood as necessary and organic members (*Gliederungen*) between the individual and the state; in which the wider association was always constructed from the corporate union of narrower associations and through them first received its members; in which each narrower association, as a true and spontaneous (*originäres*) community, created of itself a special community life and its own sphere of rights, and of these surrendered to the higher association only as many as this higher association required for fulfilling its specific purpose; in which, finally, the state, in all else, is generically similar to its member associations and differs from them only in its exclusive sovereignty, which, as the highest earthly legal power, acquires a multitude of new and peculiar attributes and functions, but finds an impassible barrier in the original right of the narrower association, with the passing of which barrier it becomes void, since, through the breach of the compact of union, the members recover their right to full sovereignty. And this effective reversal of the ruling corporation theory *Althusius* accomplished equally for the public-law and for the private-law fields, and accordingly became the creator of an entirely new theory of corporations.

A century and a half passed before the natural-law theory created anew a basically similar system. In the meantime, a thorough-going federalism based upon this principle had no representative. Nevertheless, the doctrine of *Althusius* was by no means without influence, but had a lasting effect in two different directions upon the historical development of the concepts of the publicists (*publicistischer*).

In the first place, there was developed from it the word and the concept of the *composite state. Hoenonius,* who always depended upon *Althusius,* accepting the federal idea, characterized that state formed out of several cities or elevated to the *"Regnum"* or *"Imperium,"* as distinguished from the *"Respublica simplex"* existing from one city, as *"Respublica composita." Christopher Besold* took over this idea of a *"Civitas composita,"* but, since he stood aloof from the rest of the federal idea, he limited the term to the case, which was as thoroughly distinct from the state composed of *Gemeinde* and corporations as from *Bunde* and personal unions, in which several *"gentes"* with different *"leges"* were still bound to *"unum corpus politicum"* with *"unum imperium."* While he cited and kept before his eyes the German Empire as the chief example of this sort of *"Civitas composita,"* he expressly characterized this state form as a state created out of states, in which *"majestas"* belongs exclusively to the whole and the members have the character of subordinate and relative state creatures. Along this line he wrote his own dissertation *"de statu Reipublicae subalterne,"* and thoroughly developed therein with special attention to the German territories the concept of an under-state not sovereign, to be sure, and in so far not properly analogous, but otherwise analogous to the sovereign over-state, while, in a number of other treatises, he considered other narrower associations as merely corporative members of the simple state. This idea of the state of states, first set forth in this form by *Besold,* was developed forty years later by *Ludolp Hugo* in a more penetrating and systematic fashion, when he developed, on a similar base, the idea of a theoretical division of state power between the sovereign over-state and the dependent member-states, and made use of this for the construction of the *"duplex regimen"* which existed in the German Empire. Since then the notion of the composite state has never completely disappeared from theory. To be sure, although many Empire publicists accepted the doctrine as formulated by *Hugo,* and *Leibnitz* gave it an interpretation approaching still closer to the modern formation of the *Bundesstaat* concept, yet the doctrine was badly shaken by the heavy attacks which *Samuel Pufendorf* directed against it, with the weapons of a strict theory of sovereignty, at the same time founding his own systematic doctrine of the *"Systemata Civitatum"* which in permanence and organization extends beyond the simple *"foedus."* But if *Pufendorf* declared it unthinkable that a state could contain states within itself, and for this reason recognized only the personal union and the pure *Staatenbund* as normal forms of associations of states, still he had to admit that in life intermediate organizations intervened and specifically that the German Empire occupied a central position between a system of states and a unitary state. He himself, to be sure, considered every "irregularity" of this sort as a pernicious constitutional error, and for exactly this reason characterized the German Empire as a monstrosity to be corrected only by development into a proper state system. Many publicists joined him in unqualified rejection of the *Bundesstaat* concept, whereupon those who did not care to follow him in labeling as a monster the still respected corpse of the Empire had only the choice between two equally violent escapes: either to construe the Empire as a simple *Staatenbund,* or to return to the old conception of the Empire as a unitary state. But several influential writers, who in other respects accepted *Pufendorf's* dogmas and terminology, led the concept of *"Systema Civitatum irregulare,"* especially realized in the German Empire, imperceptibly back to the *"Respublica composita,"* in which the irregularity in theory remained only as a characteristic added for the sake of academic doctrine. Indeed *Hert,* while in other respects reproducing *Pufendorf's* categories, vigorously urged the full recognition of an intermediate category constructed like *Hugo's Bundesstaat* between the decentralized unitary state and the *Staatenbund.* And so when from the middle of the eighteenth century the above-mentioned change in the concept of sovereignty and particularly the doctrine of a division of power won recognition, the path was cleared also for the revival and development of the *Bundesstaat* concept. Indeed, the concept of the composite state was not only accepted again by the public-law commentators in special application to the German Empire, but was also occasionally accepted in general form by the natural-law theory and was developed by *Nettelbladt* into a formal system of general *Bundesstaat* theory. Finally, with the ground so cleared, after *Pütter* in 1777 had completed his well-known, detailed new basis for the *Bundesstaat* construction of positive German public law, the concept of the state composed of states was accepted almost without question in regard to the withered corpse of the Empire; then, in our century, it began its great march of victory and entered upon its rich and diversified modern process of internal development.

Just as the *Bundesstaat* idea grew in historical continuity from the federalistic idea as reproduced upon a natural-law basis by *Althusius,* in the same way the historical development of the public-law concept in a second direction was permanently fixed by him. For through *Althusius'* detailed and consistent formulation of the principle of social contract there was also injected into the

theory of the *corporative composition* of the state an element of
thought which was not to be entirely suppressed by all the absolutistic pressure, and which finally unfolded a natural-law association theory which directly prepared the way for the modern
idea of *Gemeinde* and *Genossenschaft* freedom.

Whenever the deduction of the state was strictly drawn from
the social contract, a similar deduction of the *Gemeinde* and
Genossenschaften could not be avoided. But thus the narrower
associations were declared to be of equal birth with the state.
There was ascribed to them an original community life that was
no mere gift from the state, even though it was subject to state
sanction and limitation. Indeed, a conception of this sort found its
way into many political systems. But it was *Grotius* above all who
expressed it in a manner strongly reminiscent of *Althusius*. For
he not only thoroughly emphasized the similar genesis and nature
of each narrower *"consociatio"* with the *"societas perfectissima"*
realized in the state, but also conceived the composite organization
of the state as an eternal federation (*societas immortalis et per-
petua*) of its member-associations. From this he inferred that
the *"totum corpus"* could not alienate its *imperium* over a *"pars
populi"* without the consent of that part, and that the part, on the
other hand, although regularly just as incapable of effecting a
one-sided dissolution, still had the right in the exceptional case to
tear itself loose just as soon as there remained no other obvious
means of maintaining itself. But that the *"jus partis ad se tuen-
dum"* was greater than the *"jus corporis in partem"* he demonstrated with the characteristic argument: *"quia pars utitur jure
quod ante societatem initam habuit, corpus non item."*

Nor could *Hobbes* avoid the consequence of the contract-idea:
namely, to construe the *"Systemata subordinata,"* which he had developed in detail and recognized as necessary and useful, as associational institutions analogous to the state, which, in spite of the
necessity for state sanction or permission, had, in the last analysis,
a spontaneous existence. Nevertheless, he knew how to accomplish
at this point in an epoch-making manner a turn towards sharpest
absolutism. For when, in opposition to *Althusius* and *Grotius,* he
constructed his state from the contract of isolated and naked
individuals without an intermediate step, and had the individuals
completely and explicitly surrender to the state their power no

matter how created, there might still dwell within the individuals the ability to form associations, but there was irrevocably lost to them the ability to organize an association with any social power whatever over themselves. Power was no longer theirs; only the almighty state had power to grant. *Hobbes* then taught that in each *"Systema subordinatum"* all *"potestas"* was loaned and allotted by the state, that the power of representation which stamped the association as a civil-law person was an overflow of the omnipotence of the state, and that the competence of all corporative organs was bounded simply by the authority guaranteed them by the state and not by the commission of the collectivity subjected to them. Where it was otherwise, there arose a "state within a state" (*"civitas in civitate"*) which was incompatible with the doctrine of sovereignty.

When such absolutists as set out from a different basis also agreed with these results found by *Hobbes,* then these results as well as the argument were introduced into the natural-law state theories dominated by the doctrine of contract. Even the liberal *Hüber,* who, as the practical result of a certain independence, did not turn aside from the *Gemeinde* and corporations but considered them with particular partiality and thoroughness, not only fully accepted the concession-theory in principle, but also deduced every power of the officers to represent a narrower association from the authority bestowed upon them directly by the sovereign; and he was able, therefore, in spite of the similar associational basis, to define the difference in nature between state and *universitas,* in that the *"persona"* of the former came from the people, that of the latter from the state power. It was of the greatest significance, moreover, that *Pufendorf* also, although he sketched a general theory of *"personae morales compositae"* which was rich in new ideas, and presented this as a foundation equally valid for the state and for all associations, still attached himself unreservedly to *Hobbes* in his theoretical conception of the public-law relationships of the narrower associations. *Thomasius* proceeded in a similar fashion, when at the same time he emphasized strongly, on the one hand, the difference between the simple *"societas aequalis"* and the association armed with power over its members, and, on the other hand, specifically called attention to the fact that the *Gemeinde* as mere *"partes Reipublicae"* were no special steps in association and for that reason had been completely ignored by *Aristotle,* but that the *Genossenschaften* as *"societates arbitrariae"* found no place whatever in natural law. In an even more striking manner, *Hert* connected with a pure associational construction of all moral personality the doctrine that each narrower community was *per se* a mere *"societas aequalis,"* and received every power from the state alone. And from this point he continued that, whereas the state through its ruler was a body with a soul, the *universitas* lacked this soul, and existed only as a *"persona mystica"*: *"quoniam universitas pars est tantum civitatis et quicquid juris spirituumve habet, accepit concessu vel expresso vel tacito compotum summae potestatis."* And in the same circle of thought moved the systematizers of general state law who had come under the influence of *Pufendorf.*

Against this development of the natural-law state theories, *positive jurisprudence* stepped forward in the seventeenth and even in the eighteenth century as the conservative guardian of established corporative rights. But jurisprudence entered the strife with the old weapons of the private-law conception on the one hand and the doctrine of privileges on the other, and had not a remote thought of the resurrection in principle of the idea of associational community life. On the whole, it was only privileged corporations, not the corporative idea, that jurisprudence worried about. So much the more complete was the victory of the opposing tendency, pushing forward continuously from the middle of the seventeenth century, which filled itself with the spirit of absolutistic natural-law doctrine, and showed step by step the consequences of this doctrine in application to the positive-law relations of corporations generally, and to the various traditional historic species of union in particular. Ever more forcefully did jurisprudence develop the transformation of the privileged corporation into the public-law state institution artificially endowed with private-law subjectivity. Ever more definitely was it taught that every acquired privilege became untenable as soon as it contradicted the *"salus publica,"* but that public well-being demanded the concentration by all means of all political power in the hands of the sovereign. Ever more bluntly was the theory of *"persona ficta"* developed for the sphere of powers still left to the corporation in its own right, and from the perpetual minority of this *"persona*

ficta" was deduced the inseparable over-guardianship of the state.
All this, moreover, could be generally supported because in regard
to the imperial union the federal conception conquered, and after
the Peace of Westphalia, at all events, the territories were considered as states which were simply different in character from
narrower communities, and to which exactly so much of right
accrued as was taken from the *Gemeinde* and corporations.

But the natural-law state theory by no means remained fixed
during the eighteenth century at the point it had reached, but
rather developed in two opposite directions, one of which was
the centralistic-atomistic point of view which finally achieved the
theoretical denial of all intermediary members between the sovereign individual and the sovereign generality; the other developed
out of the individualistic-collectivistic conception the principle
of free association and with its help undertook a rebuilding of
the corporative structure.

The first of these tendencies was especially victorious in
France, where first *Turgot,* in the famous article in which he
justified the right of the state to break up every *"corps par-
ticulier,"* openly pronounced that between the sacred human rights
of the individual and the sovereignty of the civil association embodied in the state there was no room for the original right of existence of narrower associations. There also *Rousseau,* drawing
the final consequence here as everywhere else, generally rejected
every *"association partielle"* as a breaking and falsifying of the
general will. There finally the Revolution, after numerous con-
troversies over the relation of state parts to the state whole, in
theory and practice nevertheless employed the unitary doctrine to
order the concept of the organic corporation out of the world, and
to set in its place the concept of the division (*Abteilung*) organized from the center out, within the totality of free and equal
individuals united into a unitary collective body. Moreover, in
Germany also an approach to this tendency, victorious in France,
took place in the second half of the eighteenth century in pro-
portion as the ideas of avowed despotism were propagated. Here
also every security of traditional rights disappeared more and
more before the natural rights, which alone were regarded as
eternal and sacred; more and more there appeared as natural
rights merely human rights on the one hand and the sovereignty

of the civil community on the other; more and more these great struggling principles were fused together in the war of extermination against the independent intermediary members, in which the state discerned an unbearable limitation upon its sovereignty and the individual an annoying chain upon his freedom and equality. Under the influence of the French Revolutionary doctrine, even *Fichte* was unable to rise to a higher vision at precisely this point; nor did *Kant* know how to restore through a new, living principle of social unification the corporation which he had identified with the foundation (*Stiftung*) and radically destroyed. And finally the theory and practice of the states of the Confederation of the Rhine realized, in their dealings with narrower associations, the most faithless and thoughtless copy of the French model.

Meanwhile, however, and also in Germany, the natural-law theory of the state was developed in another direction, in which it supported the idea of free association at every step and finally approached again the associational structure of *Althusius,* built up from below. The way was prepared for this process of development particularly by the ever fuller unfolding of a general, natural theory of association founded upon the doctrine of the social contract, which placed all communities, including the state, under the same classification, and construed them according to the same scheme. If, then, every original power might be denied the narrower communities through the sharp differentiation of *Societas aequalis* and *inaequalis,* and the influence of the state power might be carried deep into their inner life, it was nevertheless by no means unimportant that in principle the corporation was ever more strongly represented as a community similar to the state, arising out of free association, and existing for itself; that the *Gemeinde* particularly stepped again into possession of an original sphere of rights; that, in the case of the church, the collegial system, though often in a purely territorial sense, began its victorious march. In this sense, *J. H. Boehmer,* although he denied again practically all independent associational life, partly on the ground of the derivation of all power from the state, partly on the ground of a precise delineation of the concept of corporative authority, may still be named as one of the first to have again advanced in theory the thought of the associational nature of all narrower communities. Then with *Wolff* and his followers, general natural social theory began to be of some practical service to the *Gemeinde* and corporations. But the decisive change was accomplished by *Nettelbladt*, since he on the one hand postulated a natural-law sphere of existence for the narrower association as well as for the individual and the state and hence ascribed to it original social rights (*jura originaria, ex natura societatis consequentia, socialia sive collegialia*), preceding all acquired rights (*jura contracta*), and parallel with innate individual rights; and, on the other hand, counted among these social rights, based upon themselves, a *"potestas"* of the generality over the members, for all cases, including the *societas aequalis*. *Nettelbladt* was thereby placed in a position to draw up a system of social organization on the basis of free association, which in many respects reproduced the ideas of *Althusius*. In a similar manner and in other respects, in the German natural-law theory the tendency toward constructing the social body from the bottom up, toward giving each community restricted in subject or place a complete position as an association arising from itself, and toward introducing the state only at the end as the overtowering spire—where, to be sure, its *"jura majestatica"* often almost crushed out again the *"jura collegialia"*—began more and more to prevail.

This tendency, developed in the German natural-law theory, exercised an influence upon political ideology which is not to be underestimated. While the greatest French proponent of the intermediate corporate community, *Montesquieu,* was unable to conceive of the corporation, which he had declared indispensable only in the monarchy, otherwise than in the sense of the embodied privilege of an estate, *Justus Möser,* in Germany, entered the lists with intense zeal for the established structure of estates, with intense hostility against the standardizing and leveling tendency of natural law, but still in a free and modern spirit in behalf of the corporation; and certainly the great man was inspired more than he himself realized by the ideas developed by the natural-law theory, for he not only wanted to make the autonomous and independent associational organization of every sphere of life the foundation of the state, but also gave expression to his thoughts on the power of free association in often prophetic fashion. Then towards the end of the century *Schlözer* was already preaching the freest right of association and declaring in regard to all, but especially religious associations: "The great community must not only allow them to exist, it must also protect them; the ideas and dealings of the single gild concern it not at all, so long as they are not contrary to the civil compact." Even *Wilhelm von Humboldt* advanced the notion of the subordination of the state community and considered that wherever free association extended this had preference by far over state institutions.

Like political theory, positive jurisprudence, since the last decade of the previous century, had been so thoroughly affected by the natural-law doctrine of associations that the general structure of the Roman corporation theory threatened to crumble away.

And who can fail to recognize the spirit of natural-law social doctrine in the associational system rising from below which was developed in the great work of legislation of the Prussian state, accomplished in a fashion so liberal-minded for its time?

This natural-law association theory was, to be sure, like the state theory growing from it, still arranged individualistically and mechanically. Since it wiped out every sharp boundary between *societas* and *universitas*, it generally agreed internally with the concept of an associational compact forcefully binding individual with individual, and externally, with the concept of a "moral person" displaying the totality of united individuals as a collective unity. It was therefore in its innermost nature and its last goal foreign and even hostile to the historic and organic impetus of corporate life, to the idea of a collective personality outlasting changing generations of individuals, and of a community fusing the fragments into a higher unity of life. Indeed, *Wilhelm von Humboldt* expressed the innermost feeling of this school, when he declared it most desirable to set up corporations through freely formed and freely dissolved association of individuals, and so, by avoidance of every permanent binding of free isolated individuals and of every effect upon future generations, to weave, in the place of corporative "chains," social "bonds"; when he proposed to avoid every disadvantage, regardless of the privileges, which might come simply from the unity of the dangerous moral person, by a specific legislative declaration "that every moral person or association is established for no further purpose than the uniting of its present members, and therefore nothing can prevent these from dissolving at pleasure through the use of associational power and means, by a majority vote"; when, finally, he condemned all special principles of law dealing with corporations and foundations as superfluous, since the principles of contract and testamentary action were fully sufficient.

Yet this tendency, which was by no means pushed to such consequences everywhere, won lasting distinction by its emphasis of the free association, not only as opposed to the outworn privileged corporation, but also as opposed to the centralizing-atomistic tendency. And from it indispensable elements of thought certainly descended to the modern world, through whose acceptance the historic-organic concept of the intermediate community, so forcefully developed in our century, was ever more qualified to overcome the opposing centralistic and individualistic elements.

APPENDIX C.

THE NATURE OF HUMAN ASSOCIATIONS.[1]

.... I invite you today to consider a basic problem which raises a questioning head in jurisprudence: a problem, however, which has its roots in all sciences and is not without relation to natural sciences. I am prompted to this by a certain inner compulsion, for this problem has been the point of departure for my intellectual life's work and remains the central point of that work. It is the problem of human associational unity: the question of the nature of those associations, so different from each other, which we place under the generic classification of social bodies, and to which we thereupon ascribe a common characteristic which the noble institutions of state and church share with the most loosely-formed association and the most lowly *Gemeinde.*

Jurisprudence is forced to deal with the nature of human society for two reasons. In the first place, law is a part of social life. Jurisprudence, therefore, can not deal with the origin of law without going back to the society that creates it; it must answer the question that promptly arises: whether the state alone creates law, whether other agencies create law in the form of autonomous principles, or whether unorganized society also creates law in the form of customary law. Further, it must ascertain the position in relation to society of single individuals active in the creation of law. Finally, it must clarify the relation between the internal and external sides of law and between the verdict of reason and the act of will which precede the creation of law. Accordingly, if jurisprudence follows up the life of law, it is forced at every step to examine into the function of law in the whole life of society and into the relations of this function to other functions of social life. Obviously such a task can not be achieved without positing a definite conception of the nature of human society in general.

---

[1] *Das Wesen der menschlichen Verbände,* inaugural address upon assuming *Rektorat* at the University of Berlin, 15 Oct., 1902 (1902).

Yet a conception of society is not an independent goal for jurisprudence, but only a means to achieve an understanding of the nature of law. Therefore I shall not pursue this subject today. I
shall turn rather to the other point at which the problem of society becomes important for jurisprudence. I said above that law
is a part of social life; I must now add that the organization of
social life is a part of law. The rule of law not only comprehends
the external relations of single lives, but also regulates the life
of the state, the church, the *Gemeinde,* and the *Genossenschaft.*
And in relation to all these organizations, it is not satisfied, as it
is in the case of individuals, with setting norms for external relations. No! It also governs and penetrates their inner life. Hence
the question of the nature of associations is no longer a preliminary question for jurisprudence, but a basic question. For to
understand and evaluate that part of law which serves to organize the life of associations one must attempt to discover what it
really is that enters the realm of law at this point and gets its
organization from law. It is recognized that our positive law
treats organized communities, in so far as it recognizes them as
such, as unitary creatures to which it ascribes personality. They
are designated as "juristic persons" and, like single men, are subjects of rights and duties. So much is certain. But doubt enters
when it is asked what reality lies at the basis of this legal phenomenon. Here juristic theories disagree.

One point of view, which practically ruled for a long time, and
which is still held today by those who are fundamentally supporters of an individualistic conception of society, maintains that the
juristic person is a fiction postulated by law for specific purposes.
An imaginary unity! Something created out of thin air! Reality,
it is said, shows us only single men as subjective, self-contained
unities. Every association is but a sum of single men who stand
in a particular relation to each other. From an objective point
of view one may ascribe to it as much unity as is desired. But, in
any case, it lacks in reality that physico-spiritual unity by virtue
of which the individual is fitted by nature to be a subject of law.
The single individual has personality, because he is a free-willing
creature; associations as such can not will and can not act. Such
is reality. Remarkable! But law can not be satisfied with this
reality. It requires a unitary bearer of the complex of rights and

duties established for common interests, a central point of contact for the common sphere of power which limits the sphere of power of individuals. It therefore makes use of its privilege of enlisting in its service the ever ready means of fiction to create the subjective associational unity which it needs. The juristic person is a fictitious person! I shall not enter into every shading of this general point of view. In its strongest form, the fiction theory declares the new legal subject to be an artificial individual which takes a position as a convenient third person beside, but in complete isolation from, the associated individuals; which, however, leads a shadowy existence as a mere conceptual creature, similar in its inability to will and act to the child, or, better, to the incurable lunatic; and which achieves a borrowed capacity to act only through representation by natural persons. From other sides the poetic color of an homunculus-creation is stripped from the fiction. It is said to mean only that any impersonal institution will be treated as though it were a person. Or it is said to mean that a multiplicity is to be considered in law as a unity. But however the fiction may be veiled or diverted, it still maintains that the personality of an association comes into existence only by a juristic artificiality, by virtue of which the association assumes in law an attribute which it lacks in reality.

Theoretically, sober protest had to arise against such a point of view. The cry sounded: Away with the juristic person! What is the meaning in the world of law—which is still a world of reality—of this bloodless apparition, of this scarecrow dressed like a man standing beside physical men? Let us respect reality! But what was one to put in the place vacated? One found a purposive capacity without a subject; and thereby one removed only the fiction. For since a right without a subject is a contradiction, the purpose itself appeared as a fictitious subject. And therefore one ventured the last step. If individual persons alone are well-endowed unities, then they alone can be subjects of rights and duties. All social law is at best the law common to many, and all social organization but a far-reaching net of relations between individuals. The individualist theory, if consistent, could not, of course, simply strike out of private law the concept of the juristic person which it had legally established there; but it could reduce the concept to the level of a technical instrument, a generic term, a shortened formula. For public law, there was an open road. Thus single adherents of this point of view in state law opened their war of annihilation against the concept of state personality, in which the more recent public law had thought to have found its central point. Indeed, the notion of the *persona ficta* must prove particularly inadequate when applied to the subject of the highest earthly authority. Shall the claim in the last instance to the lives and property of physical men be granted to a conceptual creature of the imagination? Shall the king occupy his noble position as the trustee of a person which, like a mentally-deficient, is unqualified to care for its own interest? Shall the imperial court speak the law in the name of a shadow? Yet so the theory implies! If there are no true persons except individuals, then the state, if it is a person, can only be a fictitious person. But then the victory seems to go to those who ban the concept of state personality from public law. The state is a condition, perhaps also a legal relation, perhaps also an object of law; a subject of law it is not. The subject of state authority is rather the ruler alone, be the ruler a single individual or a collectivity of individuals. Other subjects are set up to represent the ruler; in the constitutional state there are also subjects designated for obligatory cooperation in exercising the state authority. Fixed rights are guaranteed the citizens of the state as against the ruler. But the unity of a legally organized multiplicity comes into being exclusively through the position of the ruler as subject; beyond the ruler there is no other subject.

Is this, then, the final conclusion of wisdom? Or does not this logical development of the individualistic conception of society in public law bring us close to the suspicion that the basis of the whole structure is untenable? Indeed, it seems to me that the attempt to eliminate state personality must necessarily come to naught. For to achieve it is historically impossible. It would involve a retrogression in public law and a step backward in culture. . . . It was only with untold labor and not without frequent retracing of steps that the independent personality of the organized whole was placed at the apex of thought. State personality was always tending to disappear into either a sovereign ruler or a sovereign people. The adherents of absolutism taught what Louis XIV brought into the brief formula: *"L'état c'est moi."*

To this the apostles of popular sovereignty countered that the
state was contained in the sum of ·citizens. But finally there appeared, steadily stronger and more clear, the ·idea· that the true
subject of sovereignty was the immortal state. . It filled the soul
of Frederick the Great when he, the absolute monarch, uttered the·
unforgettable words that he was the first servant of the state. It ·
became the guiding star of jurisprudence when jurisprudence
created modern public law with all its consequences out of the
lasting, invisible unity of the state, the same through changing
generations and even changing constitutions. Its creative force
was more completely unfolded when, in the constitutional state of
the nineteenth century, popular organs were called into integrated
cooperation in the exercise of state authority. Penetrating all our
public institutions and deeply rooted in the general consciousness, it
forms an essential part of our culture today, of which no logical
deduction can deprive us.

And so corporative persons will not yield. We should have
to endure them even if they were phantoms. Is it not, however,
possible that their tough resistance demonstrates that they are by
no means ghostly shadows, but living creatures? That law, when
it treats organized associations as persons, is not disregarding reality, but giving reality more adequate expression? Is it not possible that human associations are real unities which receive through
legal recognition of their personality only what corresponds to
their real nature?

I, with many others, answer, yes! And it seems to me that
everyone must so answer who has broken with the individualist
concept of society and who pictures the human community as
a life of a higher order composed of individual lives.

Since the beginning of the science of state and law, this view,
for which every community is simply an aggregate of individuals,
has been opposed by another, which sees in social bodies independent wholes with a nature of their own. This conception held
a foremost place in classical philosophy. The social theory of the
Christian Middle Ages was saturated with it. It did not die out,
but has been firmly pushed out of sight since the triumph of the
natural-law social theory with its deduction of all corporate existence from the free union of individuals. It has arisen with renewed strength during the transformation which political and legal

UNIVERSITY OF WISCONSIN STUDIES

thinking has experienced since the turn of the eighteenth century. To measure the significance of the movement, one may follow in its different stages the transition accomplished by Fichte in his social theory from pure natural-law individualism to the notion of the reality and original value of the community. Since then the scientific conviction of the reality of the community has spread out continually. It has broken its way in philosophic reflection in general from Hegel to Wundt, in the teaching of the historical school of law, in the young sciences of cultural history, of social psychology, and of general sociology. The triumph of the idea of evolution in the natural sciences has worked to strengthen it. To be sure, not only is the enemy's camp not disarmed, but in the ranks of the adherents of the social point of view there is little unity to be seen. Theories of the reality of super-individual unities, sometimes proceeding from metaphysical speculation, sometimes concocted from observation mixed with more or less imagination, have been and are extremely diverse. If, on the one hand, they were spiritualized in such measure that the reality of concrete communities (*universitates*) could be thrown together with the reality of an abstract conception of organism (*universalia*) fashioned upon Plato's doctrine of ideas, and could thereupon be involved in the overthrow of realism by nominalism,—on the other hand, they were so thoroughly materialized that it became possible to treat social bodies as purely natural bodies, something like coral-reefs formed by many single polyps. Still it remains to be noticed that from such opposing points of view some sort of reality is ascribed to corporate unity. This does not exclude the possibility of an illusion. But it encourages us to introduce hypothetically the idea of real corporate unity into the problem of legal corporate personality.

Let us suppose then that the legally organized community is a whole in which dwells a real unity, and then let us undertake to determine from the point of view of law how this whole must be constructed if reality is to be mirrored in law. Law attributes personality to the association. Then, like the individual, it must be a physico-spiritual living unity which has a will and can translate its will into action. But law orders and dominates the inner structure and life of the association. In distinction from the individual, then, it must be a living structure in which it is possible to regulate the relation of the totality to its parts by means of objective norms for human will.

These are the basic ideas from which the so-called organic theory has sprung. They run through the political theory of the classical period, and the social theory of the Middle Ages; they are found in every attempt to combat the final atomistic-mechanical conclusion contained within the natural-law line of reasoning; but it is only in the nineteenth century that they have come to scientific development under the influence of the new ideas about human social life.

The organic theory views the state and other associations as social organisms. It asserts the existence of a collective organism, whose parts are human beings, which is above individual organisms. Then it classifies under this category only phenomena in which it discovers common characteristics. But since the organic concept came originally from the nature of individual life, the theory naturally tends to draw comparisons between the social organism and the individual organism. This comparison is of ancient standing, and has always impressed itself upon unreflecting human consciousness. It has left indelible marks upon our common speech, and is even the basis of technical legal expressions. . . .

Comparison, however, always remains a mere instrument of perception. It can explain but not define. If it is used to draw, from agreement in single characteristics of the things compared, conclusions about agreement in other characteristics which would not otherwise be recognized, then it becomes a source of error. The organic theory has not been entirely free of extravagance of this sort. . . .

The critics of the organic theory emphasize its exaggerations. They are right when they combat these exaggerations. But they are wrong when they see in such exaggerations the unavoidable consequences of the comparison between natural and social organisms. Rightly understood, nothing more is claimed by the comparison than that we recognize in the social body the unity of life of a whole arising out of separate parts,—such a unity as we do not find elsewhere except in natural living creatures. We do not forget that the inner structure of a whole whose parts are men must be of such a quality that natural structures can not serve as its model; we do not forget that there takes place here a spiritual unification which is established, given form, put into operation, and dissolved by psychically motivated action; that here the domain of natural science ends and the domain of philosophy and psychology begins. But we view the social whole, like the individual organism, as a living structure, and classify the collective community together with the individual creature under the general concept of living creatures. Whatever of the figurative occasionally accompanies this arises partly out of the need for clarity, partly from limitations of speech. All intellectual progress has been accomplished with the aid of imagery. Our most abstract concepts are born from pictures. We may also make use of imagery in science as long as we keep the fact in mind, and do not take the picture for the object itself. But so long as we have at our command for the designation of the object itself only expressions whose pictorial impression has not been polished down, we must be careful to separate the conceptual content from the pictorial admixture.

Nevertheless, as long as it holds to this approach, the organic theory will be charged by its opponents with over-stepping the boundaries of science. The acceptance of living unities beyond the living unity of the individual is mysticism. Our sensual perception shows us only single men. He who ascribes to invisible associations an independent life introduces a supernatural element into visible reality.

This argument, however frequently we meet it, is, for all its shallowness, unclear through and through. In the first place, it is incorrect to say that sensual perception tells us nothing of the existence of associations. For corporate life plays a role in the physical world which appears in outward form. We see a regiment marching to ringing music; we notice voters who cast their votes into the urn; at a public demonstration we are roughly pushed back by a squad of policemen;—and we know immediately by this and a hundred other sensual impressions that things are happening which have to do with the continuation of the life of the state. To be sure, we always see only single parts of the body of the state. While we may appraise the body of a single individual as a whole, we can not look upon the physical nature of the state as a whole. Art can not, therefore, portray the state physically as it can in-- dividual men; it gropes for a symbol and presents to us the noble figure of a woman as Germania or Borussia. Yet there is here no objection to be found against the reality of the social body. For the inability of the senses to comprehend the total impression proves nothing against the external objectivity. We have no doubt that the earth is a globular body, although we can experience directly only a tiny section of it.

On the other hand, one thing is undeniably certain: however much or little we may see of associations, their living unity we can not see! What the senses bring to our attention is always bodies in motion. If we interpret these as the working of a living unity, then we reveal the invisible by means of the visible, and when we attribute personality to any association whatever, we relate the quality of being a fixed subject with this invisible unity. And with single men the case is no different. Human unity of life also escapes sensual perception. Human personality also is an attribute ascribed to this invisible unity which is disclosed only by its activity. It is a gross error to say that one can see with his own eyes this individual personality. The personality of a man remains the same when his physical body changes; the personality suffers no division or damage when the physical body loses a member. At any rate, the senses are sufficient to recognize how far a man is a self-sufficient individual and how far he is involved as a member of a social group. Wherever we have to deal with the notion of a unit distinct from the sum of its parts acting in a living fashion, we are moving in an invisible world. But do we thereby forsake the firm ground of reality? Is the real that which is perceptible to the senses? He who maintains this has not crossed the threshold of philosophic reflection.

Finally there is raised against the organic theory the objection that, by introducing an unclear concept, it beclouds rather than clarifies what it seeks to explain. For the nature of an organism is itself an unsolved mystery. Natural science has sought in vain to explain the nature of the natural organism. Thus social science gains little or nothing by adopting for its use this unknown some-thing-or-other.

This objection also is invalid. That which we recognize as real must find a place in our rational world, even though its real nature is unexplained and perhaps impossible of explanation. The puzzle of the organism is identical with the puzzle of life. We do not know what life really is. But we can not for that reason exclude the concept of life from science. For we know that life exists. Moreover, we can describe and delimit the phenomena of life. In this way we form a concept of life with which we operate in natural science and philosophy. But wherever we assume life we find a bearer of life which exhibits certain characteristics. We notice that this bearer is an organized unit containing differentiated parts, and maintaining itself by the purposive cooperation of those parts; and that this unity, constant in spite of changes in its parts, and working together with the parts, is not identical with the sum of its parts. The real nature of this unity in multiplicity is hidden from us. But we can not for that reason strike the subject of living institutions out of our science. For it is certain that they exist. Furthermore, we are in a position to ascertain and describe the specific characteristics of this bearer of life. Accordingly, we construct a concept of this bearer of life, and for this concept use the term "organism" as referring to the peculiar structure of the experienced whole. This concept is just as suitable scientifically as any other concept that is reached by accurate abstraction from the known facts in the case, and likewise expresses a reality. Its legitimacy does not depend upon the ability to explain the reality upon which it is based. We have, therefore, the right and the obligation to employ this concept for social units in so far as we recognize in them unitary bearers of life.

But what about such recognition? Can the organic theory not only dispose of the objections of its opponents but also bring forth positive proof for its scientific justification? Can it demonstrate that living social units exist?

Direct proof for the existence of living social units is not to be found. But neither is the individual living unit directly demonstrable. We may well, however, infer indirectly the existence of such units from their actions. The force of conviction in this sort of proof will certainly not be the same for everyone. Here one's *Weltanschauung* plays a role. But even the bases of scientific comprehension which seem most substantial are only well-grounded hypotheses.

It is, in the first place, experience which moves us to an acceptance of active social units. By observation of social institutions within which our life runs its course, but, above all, by exploring the history of mankind, we are shown that the actions of peoples and other communities fashion the world of forceful relationships and produce material and spiritual cultures. Since communities arise from individuals, this all occurs in and through individuals. But the individuals, in so far as their activity is connected with the social institution, are controlled by physical and intellectual influences which flow from their membership in the institution. To be sure, we observe that single, dominant individuals play creative roles, and by qualities which come from themselves alone transform the community. But this is possible only when the community coöperates and takes over as its own what is introduced by the individual. It is possible to hold widely differing opinions upon the question of how far the active influence of the whole or of the individual is responsible for great changes in social life. But whether one embraces a one-sided cult of hero-worship or revels in a one-sided collective picture of history, still one can never overlook the fact of a continual interaction between the two factors. At all events, the community is something active. But then the activities which we must attribute to the community are such that they can not be explained as arising from a mere sum of individual forces. For they can not be produced in part by any isolated individual, so that the whole result might be considered similar in kind to the partial results and only quantitatively larger; on the contrary, they are of a particular type. Organization of force, law, morals, national economy, speech—these are phenomena which promptly come to mind. The active community, therefore, can not be identified with the sum of its active parts; it must rather be a whole with a unity of life above its individuals. We are still in the domain of external experience when we induce the existence of a real social unity from the facts of cultural history. And we are justified in applying the concept of such a unity, induced by abstracting the real content of our findings, as a scientific basic concept in the whole field of social science.

Moreover, what we learn by external experience is verified by internal experience. For we find the reality of the community in our personal consciousness as well. The association of our ego with a social institution of a higher order is a personal experience for us. We feel ourselves to be self-sufficient beings, but we also feel ourselves to be parts of a whole which lives and acts within us. Were we to think away our membership in a particular people and state, a religious community and a church, a professional group, a family, and numerous other societies and associations, we should not recognize ourselves in the miserable remainder. But when we think over all this, it becomes clear that it is not a matter merely of external chains and bonds which bind us, but rather a matter of psychological relations which, reaching deep within us and integrating us, form constituent elements of our spiritual being. We feel that part of the impulse which determines our action comes from the community which permeates us. We become conscious that we are living a social life. If then we fashion from our inner experience the certainty of the reality of our being, this certainty is not based solely upon the fact that we form individual living entities, but also upon the fact that we are parts of a higher living entity. The higher living entity can not, to be sure, be found in our own consciousness. For since we are only parts of the whole, we can not contain the whole within ourselves; and so from inner experience we can learn directly only of the existence and not of the nature of the social unit. Indirectly, however, we can conclude from the effects of the community upon ourselves that the social entities are of physico-spiritual nature. For these effects exist in physically-mediated psychic incidents. For this reason we speak not only of social bodies and their members, but also of the soul of the people, the national consciousness, popular conviction and popular will, of class spirit, of fraternity spirit, of family spirit, and so forth. We designate thereby very lively psychic forces, of whose reality we are not the least conscious when, making use of our individuality, we revolt against them. Self-observation may convince us every day of the existence of these spiritual forces. But there are hours in which the community spirit manifests itself with primitive force in almost tangible form and so fills and dominates our inner being that we are scarcely conscious of our single existence as such. Such a sacred hour I experienced here in Berlin *Unter den Linden* on. 15 July, 1870.

So the scientific justification of the concept of the real physico-spiritual unity of human societies seems to me to be well established. Beyond that, scientific perception does not go. The secret of the real nature of these living unities remains undiscovered. Here imagination or faith may enter. The metaphysical necessity for a unitary picture of the world will not die, and there will always spring up new attempts to solve the riddle of the universe by a mixture of knowledge and faith. The single sciences dare not become involved in speculation upon the transcendent. Their task is to explore with methods adapted to their nature the basic relationship of phenomena in their own territories, and to penetrate to the last discernible effective factor. Therefore the concept of living social entities will play unequal roles in the separate sciences which belong to the larger unit of cultural or social science. In so far as the phenomena handled by each science go back to effective social forces, it will have to turn to this concept and develop it to the extent that its particular task requires.

For the problem of jurisprudence with which I began and to which I now return, only those communities come under consideration whose unity is expressed in a legal organization. For they alone are called and entitled to enter law as persons. Numerous communities of very energetic effective force are thus excluded, and especially, since the folk becomes a person only as the state, that folk-community which is without a state or which extends beyond the state. Its living social unity, the nationality, is, to be sure, a powerful influence in law, as well as in speech, morals, and all spiritual and material culture, and therefore, demands attention in jurisprudence. But it does not appear among the subjects of law. The community of nations also creates law, without being a subjective unity before the law. The same is true of the religious community, in so far as it does not, as a church, become a person. It is true of class, professional, and interest communities, of political and social parties, in so far as these do not come together into organized societies. But wherever a community appears as a legally organized unit, there arises the legal question of whether and with what validity the living social unit shall be recognized as a collective person. And wherever a collective person appears, jurisprudence is faced with the task of comprehending, regulating, and developing the legal principles governing the external and internal life of the society and serving as the expression of the physico-spiritual living unity of the social organism.

Is it then not relatively immaterial for jurisprudence how the problem of the juristic person is solved? Are we simply discussing a theoretic, academic conflict, the conclusion of which is not necessary for a purely juristic understanding of law, and which is meaningless for the practical formulation and administration of law?.

By no means! The whole systematic structure of law, the form and content of the most important legal concepts, and the solution of numerous very practical single problems are dependent upon the construction of collective personality. And the organic conception demonstrates that it alone is in a position to find what is consistent with our legal consciousness and the necessities of life. I can not go into this further today. I shall allow myself only a few suggestions.

If the law of association is a system of life for social beings, then that part of the law of association which regulates the inner life of societies must be basically different from all other law, which regulates the external relations of beings which it recognizes as subjects. In accordance with the twofold nature of men, who are at the same time entities in themselves and parts of higher entities, law must be divided into two great branches, which we may designate as individual law and social law. To the category of social law must be assigned state law and all other public law, but also the internal system of rules of the private collective person, which are embodied in private law. The social law must include concepts which have no counterpart in individual law. For here legal regulation is extended to a sphere which, in the case of individuals, can not be regulated.

Here law can determine by rules the construction of the living whole from its parts and the part that its unity is to play in the conglomerate, because and in so far as the inner structure of the social organism is at the same time the external life of men or of more restricted societies of men. Thus the legal concept of the constitution emerges. The construction of social bodies from the persons belonging to them is controlled by legal principles. There arises the legal concept of membership. Membership as a legal state acquires a content consisting of rights and duties; the sphere of life and action of the member-person which is claimed by the association is delineated from the sphere of the individual which still remains free; through control of its losses and gains, the incidents of entering or leaving the association become legal incidents. Further, the organization of this body is regulated by legal principles, since every member-person is allotted his position in the whole, higher and lower orders are established, classification decreed for the complex of members, a single member perhaps acknowledged as the legal head. And, above all, legal principles determine the organization by virtue of which these elements bound to the whole form a unity. In so far as law decrees that under certain conditions the living unity of the whole shall receive legal recognition through the activities of specific members or combinations of members, it stamps the concept of the organism as a legal concept. A vast complex of principles, extremely different for the different societies and often very involved, serves to establish the number and type of organs, to grant to each of them a definite sphere of activity as competence or duty, to regulate the relation of the organs among themselves, to insure their cooperation and the direction of lower organs by higher organs up to the highest organ, to define the form of procedure for exercising organic functions, and to adapt these functions to their purpose. Therefore, legal principles extend to the formation of the organ by the single person or group of persons designated for the time being to act as the organ, to the acquisition or loss of this position, and to the relation of the organic personality to the individual personality of the participants. The legal concept of the organ is of a specific type and not to be confused with the individualist concept of the representative. Here it is not a matter of a self-sufficient person being represented by another self-sufficient person. But, just as when the eye sees, or the mouth speaks, or the hand grasps, the man sees and speaks and grasps, so, when the organ functions within its proper competence, the living unity of the whole acts directly. Through the organ, then, the invisible collective person appears as a perceptive, deliberating, willing, and acting unity. The juristic person of our law is not a mute creature requiring a legal representative, but a subject acting for itself in the external world. It is capable of conducting its own affairs. It is also—and this will be stubbornly denied by the fiction theory, but is still ever more forcefully demonstrated in legal practice—capable of wrong and answerable for its offenses. But since it is a legally organized community, so here too inner spiritual incidents, in so far as they are external incidents for the persons composing the organ, are regulated by legal principles. Here law concerns itself with incidents of will in all its phases, from the first stimulus on, with the conflict of motives and the weighing of reasons, with the arriving at a decision and with its translation into action. The legal principles which deal with deliberation, voting and determination, with the unification of collective organs, with the publication and carrying out of decisions,—all these again have no counterpart in individual law. Here we are opposed by the contract theory, according to which separate subjects unite in regard to the common content of their wills, which they set up as the criterion binding their relationship. Here all agreement is simply the creation of a unitary common will out of the single wills convened for the purpose, every decision from a conflict of opinions merely the accomplishment of a unity of wills in the whole. Every unresolved conflict of organs threatens to cripple, convulse, or even destroy the social organism itself; and if a crisis of this sort is solved by the triumph of force over existing law, then here there is demonstrated the real unity, which law has not created but only organized.

Furthermore, it is characteristic of social law that it is able to formulate into legal relations the relations between a unitary whole and its parts. A legal relationship between a single individual and his members or organs is unthinkable. But, on the other hand, there are rights of collective persons in relation to their member-persons and organs, which culminate in the authority of the state, in the highest rights on earth, and which are reproduced in graduated order in every degree of collective authority down to the authority of the private club. But there are also rights of member-persons and organs in their collective person: rights to a share in the management and property of the society, rights to participation in the common will as in the right to vote, rights to a special position as member or organ which extend even to the monarch's hereditary right to rule. All such legal relations have a completely different structure from the legal relations of individual law which can exist between these same subjects as bearers of distinct free capacities, and in accordance with which even the state and the single citizen stand in relation to each other as convenient private persons. But if individual legal relations are woven into a corporate association, they experience a social-law transformation derived from a particular form of property, of non-personal rights, of responsibility, and so forth.

The birth and death of social institutions are also incidents for law which can not be construed in terms of individual-law concepts and which, therefore, open a new world of social-law concepts. For example, the free act of will which calls a collective person into being is no contract, but a creative, collective act. This holds for the founding of the North German *Bund* and the German Empire, but also no less for the foundation of every society. Accordingly, the dissolution of a social body, the disposition of its remains, and the fate of its estate are controlled by legal principles of a specific nature. Similarly there arises from the division or amalgamation of social organisms a special group of legal concepts.

A rich system of social-law norms, finally, deals with the articulation of lower social organisms into higher and finally of all into the sovereign community. Societies share in common with single individuals the ability to exist as independent wholes and at the same time as members or organs of more inclusive units. But a new world of juristic concepts is opened by the fact that even the inner life of such member or organ persons is subject to the legal influence of the collective organism.

Unendingly diverse are the types of legally organized social organisms which our cultural development has brought forth in its process of progressive differentiation and integration. Institutions which are great and small, thoroughly developed and very simple, authoritative and dependent, ancient and ephemeral, growing close to the soil and founded on wealth, devoted to a many-sided common purpose or limited to a single ideal or economic object—all are to be found in the number. It is to be taken for granted that they require not basically the same but basically different law. The state, elevated over all by its sovereign complete power, lays claim to a law of a higher order, and permits only such

communities as it considers to be public establishments to take
part to a certain degree in the prerogatives of public law. The
church, with its ideal mission, demands its own law. For territorial
communities a special system is necessary. Special sets of rules
belong to every type of public body. Private corporate law is
divided according to the diversity of purpose of the society and
further according to the wide variety of corporate forms. And
finally every single social institution sets up within its own circle
a special law corresponding to its concrete individuality. Indeed, the great collective persons whose constitutional history
forms a most important part of world history have each so constructed and reconstructed their systems that in each concrete
instance of state law or church law is to be found a special system
of legal thought. In the face of such dissimilarity, general comparison might seem to many to be unwarranted. But in natural life
the endless variety and diversity of types does not exclude the
scientific recognition of a common principle at the basis of their
structure. In the same way we believe that we recognize upon
juristic examination of social institutions a common basic principle of juristic structure that runs through all social law.

In accordance with all this, it seems to me to be certain that
the organic interpretation of societies is justified in jurisprudence.
Jurisprudence has to do with social institutions only in so far as
they are active in law, and must therefore necessarily proceed in
a one-sided fashion. For legal activity is only one side of collective life, and by no means the most important side. Jurisprudence must remain conscious of this one-sidedness. It must also
bear in mind that the active powers of the social organism come to
light beyond law in all movements of force or culture and realize
their most powerful effects independently of law, or even in opposition to law. It must, however, leave it to other sciences to un-
cover all the connections and to investigate the effective units. But
only as it receives from other branches of science information
confirming the reality of the community, will it be able continually
to maintain the claim that its recognition of the legal interpretation of this reality find consideration with every social research directed toward the core of the matter.

One thing, however, may be permitted the jurist: reference
to the ethical significance which is connected with the idea of

the real unity of the community. Only from this idea comes the
conception of the community as something of value in itself. And
only from the superior value of the whole as against the part can
there arise the moral duty of men to live for the whole, and,
if necessary, to die for it. If the people is in reality only the
sum of its present single members and the state merely an institution for the well-being of living and still unborn individuals,
then the individual may be forced to place his strength and life at
its service. But he can not be placed under a moral obligation to
do so. For the splendor of a high moral idea that has always
glorified death for the Fatherland grows pale. Why should the
individual sacrifice himself for the welfare of many other individuals who are in no way different from himself? For the
ethical relation of individual to individual the command is valid:
love thy neighbor as thyself! Upon this command alone the
extreme individualists of idealistic sentiments, such as Tolstoi,
wish to base the life of human society,—and behold, they de-
molish the state and preach anarchism! The religious complement
of the command to love thy neighbor lies in the command to love
God above all. But this applies to the Kingdom of God, which is
not of this world. But for the earthly community also it means:
love the whole more than yourself! And this can have meaning
only when the whole is something higher and of more value than
the sum of its individuals, when the community is more than a
means for the purposes of individuals, and when he who lives and
fights for the honor and the welfare, for the freedom and the
right of his people and his state lives and dies not for empty
words. . . .

APPENDIX D.

THE BASIC CONCEPTS OF STATE LAW AND THE MOST RECENT STATE-LAW THEORIES[1]

I.

In the progress of every science there occurs the necessity of developing its basic principles in a double direction. It should *clarify* basic principles and it should *deepen* them. But it is seldom that a broad spirit realizes the ideal of an harmonious and equal development in both directions. Almost always the activity of the single thinker and even complete intellectual tendencies go preponderantly into the development of one side or the other, while well-justified claims which are raised from the other side often suffer considerably. It is exactly this one-sidedness that is the basic cause for the rise of the most thorough-going *antitheses of tendencies* in the single science.

Transparent *clarity* of concept is the noble goal of each science. But when clarity is sought in a *one-sided* fashion, there is danger of the development of a one-sided *formalistic* tendency. No mortal spirit has yet penetrated to clarity in regard to the final nature of a thing; the *form* above all presents itself to us, clearly and sharply set out in indelible lines. But the form is bound to the surface of a thing, and so it appears all too soon in such an effort that the clearest is also the most superficial. The danger in this tendency lies in the fact that it considers the duty of science fulfilled when the dry material is in some way or other brought into a coherent system of logical categories. If the concepts be diluted thereby into empty and shallow forms, the thinness is transparent, the shallowness is intelligible, the formality sharply defined, and thus the desired clarity is achieved. Behind the formal solution the unsolved puzzle of real existence may swell up as mightily as

---

[1] "Die Grundebegriffe des Staatsrechts und die neuesten Staatsrechtstheorien," in *Zeitschrift für die gesammte Staatswissenschaft*, XXX (1874), pp. 153 ff., 265 ff. Section II of this article is omitted, and sections I and III are cut wherever the material is not essential to the general argument.

ever; still the outer harmony between the system of thought and the facts is preserved by rash abstraction. If at numerous places the flood of life breaks through the artificial dam which the system has built up against it in its arrangement of categories and sub-categories, the blame lies with the facts and not with the system. If research discovers hitherto unknown forces, if quite new institutions appear, the formalistic approach does not consider it a duty to broaden the concepts which have become too narrow and to re-model the system, but it devotes the most careful and painstaking labor simply to reworking the new facts, formulating and classify-ing them in order to squeeze them into the old formal structure and so be "through" with them without disturbing the closed system of concepts.

On the other side, out of the consciousness of how narrow and inadequate are the concepts at hand, of how they cling to the surface, of how little they penetrate in their abstract, logical justification of form to the nature of the thing itself, there arises a tendency which bores into the depths. But the danger in this approach lies in the fact that in the unfathomed deep rests form-lessness, confusion, darkness. All too often the bold diver brings to light, instead of the richly-suggestive concept which he hoped to create down below, only a notion, suggestive to be sure, but cloudy and confused. He strives in vain for a plastic formulation of the notion, and finally only achieves a more or less fantastic picture. In place of the empty formula appears such an ambiguous *tropus*; the simple, fixed, generally-recognized *terminus technicus* is pushed out by the symbolic word whose vague meaning can be differently interpreted for every occasion. The traditional system is recognized in its defects and finally broken as an unbearable fetter; but the promised substitute is a long time in coming, and, when it finally does come, is often sadly inadequate. Intoxicated by the mass of new viewpoints and by the glance into the mystic deep, the human spirit often lacks that conscious and energetic self-limitation which alone leads to certain mastery of the mind over material. Seeing change all about, it forgets the strict, logical following of conclusions; looking upon an unbroken chain of the past, it loses sight of theoretical bounds. The horizon seems suddenly to be infinitely widened; but ever more confused, form-less, capricious become the mental images, ever more violently the flood of material rises over the shore, as chaos breaks upon the spiritual world.

Yet, however much these tendencies may degenerate in their one-sidedness, in the end they *both* serve the progress of science. . . . Meanwhile, so long as the fight and struggle continue, the representatives of opposing tendencies too easily lose sight of the common goal. Forces, which should each be struggling against the elemental obstacles to intellectual progress, turn to fight against each other. . . . Then it is the duty of every thoughtful person to fix his gaze upon the one goal that stands above all conflicts of method in order to win a more severe judgment over himself and a more balanced judgment over his opponent!

Such an admonition is perhaps today not more necessary in any science than in the *science of law.* For here the conflict of tendencies pictured above becomes apparent in a particularly sharp manner. It seems as though this conflict, which we may label a conflict between the *formalistic* and *pragmatic* approaches, might restore the antithesis, once a catchword and now out of style, of the philosophical and historical schools. If at some time it may lead to an antithesis of two complementary methods essential to each other, still at the moment the conflict leads to incomparable and mutually antagonistic results.

The *formalistic* tendency always has a certain advantage in the science of law. In no other science does the relation to practical life point so evidently to the clear and intelligible formulation of concepts. It is for this reason that the whole so-called "juristic thought" holds close to the logical-formal approach which is characteristic of it. The jurist turns with justifiable annoyance away from all vagueness, darkness, confusion; he finds profundity and mysticism uncomfortable; what does not lend itself to definition does not exist for him. With the advantages which result from this approach are easily connected all the disadvantages of a one-sided tendency. Since all the emphasis is laid exclusively upon the logical-formal side of the concept, its inner content recedes from view. It appears as the first task to emerge, in the face of all the concrete stuff of law, with the given abstractions; with the help of certain traditional categories which have crystalized in the course of the century, to "construe juristically" the daily growing complex of living legal institutions. The fact is

overlooked that the concepts at hand with which one operates
have, like current coin, acquired the advantage of general accepta-
bility through years of circulation, but that they are still themselves but the product of abstraction from certain changeable relationships and therefore by nature neither eternal nor unchangeable. Principles of relative truth conditioned by time and place
are so easily stiffened into *dogmas* and reduced to mathematical
axioms. Before such dogmas the most penetrating criticism, capable of dissolving and destroying elsewhere, comes to a halt. One
need think, for example, only of the way in which juristic thought,
in contrast with modern commercial life, is burdened by the dogmatic formulation of concepts of property, corporation, obligation,
in the sense of the Roman law. . . .

It is very easy to shake off those material factors which find
no place in the theoretical formula with the assertion that they are
"juristically irrelevant." It is none the less pleasing in order to
protect a principle against the opposing doctrines, to resort to
the frequent and yet meaningless excuse that here the *ratio juris*
is broken by a rule of equity, that a right based "upon itself" un-
derlies in a "peculiar" manner a police measure suitable for some
purpose, or however the unpleasant fact, that any theory at all
may in real life be transformed into its opposite through exceptions, may be beautified. The fiction is used in the most comprehensive manner: indeed, in the fiction law celebrates its greatest
triumphs. And where all this fails, it is made possible with the
keenest abstraction simply to deny what really exists, to set up
what is nowhere at hand as the only "theoretical" reality. The
most recent state-law theorists have succeeded in denying special
existences as "state" now to the German Empire, now to the
single German states, simply because their previously formulated
concept of the state excluded the possibility of dividing the state
authority among several collective subjects! *Sohm* even asures us
upon the basis of several very diverse *a priori* definitions that a
church placed under the usual corporation law is "juristically *not*
a church"! And in regard to the copyright law *Gerber*, since the
law did not fit into any of the existing rubrics, maintained that
here a peculiar *right* has grown from new relationships, then
continued to the remarkable assertion that in juristic relations we
have here merely the legislative creation of a new *crime!* . . .

It is further from the spirit of the formalistic tendency to grasp the dependence between law and the *other spheres of activity* of a people, even when most external! It deserves the greatest credit for pointing out emphatically the formal independence of law from its motives and *substrata*. But it undervalues the worth which the investigation of the inner relation of law with culture, particularly with economic conditions on the one side, and with ethical points of view on the other, has for the scientific formulation of legal concepts. The excuse that all that is irrelevant for "the concept in the sense of law" easily appears here also; but that does not do away with the objection that the best proof of the soundness and utility of juristic abstractions lies in their correlation with economics and ethics.— Finally the relation between *law and jurisprudence* is disarranged in general for those under the influence of this tendency. They find the nature of law in its scientific formulation and quite forget that it has a real existence before jurisprudence and independent of it. Legal science is not satisfied with a relation to law like that of grammar to language: it does not care to discover rules, but to create them. It will not recognize life, but rule it. Its one and all is the "system" that develops from a means into an end. Instead of a living organism we get a dead formal apparatus. In spite of all the exertion of intellect and acumen, one-sided formalism ends finally in a purely external technique of law. And in concrete practice this approach leads not seldom to mere mechanical routine.

Against such one-sidedness there has for a long time been a more *pragmatic* tendency in legal science struggling to bring to notice the inner content of law, to do justice to its nature as an historical manifestation of human corporate spirit. But while this tendency, which is cleft and disunited in itself, often clings fast to its material, it falls all too readily into that error which the jurist feels the hardest and is most reluctant to excuse. True, it holds fast to the thought that legal science is not identical with law, but comes upon law and must conceive law as something existing of itself. It does not, therefore, wish to master and model life according to abstract concepts, but wishes to create abstract concepts from life. Accordingly it is thoroughly convinced of the historical conditioning of all legal concepts and of the merely

relative truth of juristic dogmas. But it is thereby too easily mis-
led into undervaluing the worth of proven formal means and
of a generally known and generally understood theoretical technique. The human intellect, incapable of comprehending the nature of the *Ding an Sich*, most certainly approaches the unattainable goal when it knows how to limit itself; he who throws aside
the restricting bonds of traditional forms without finding a satisfactory substitute, too easily loses his way in the chaotic material.
If too much material comes to expression in the concept, there
may appear instead of a concept only an indeterminate point of
view. Often enough with this tendency the strength of abstraction
is worn out in observation of concrete life. Then instead of a completely intellectual conceptual word for the expression of fermenting thoughts one finds only a symbolic, comparative turn of speech.
And thereby one is always in danger of saying more than he
wished, of opening the way for the most diverse interpretations,
and finally, of introducing a confusing phrase about which no one
has a clear thought. With the well-grounded realization that this
or that traditional formula has become too narrow for the new
legal institutions forced into it, the adherents of this approach
often free themselves, prematurely and without looking ahead, of
the traditional scheme, before a satisfactory substitute has been
assured. Recognizing the arbitrariness in most definitions, they
often substitute for these mere descriptions. They reject the
unprofitable art of that juristic construction which so often de-
generates into idle play or deceptive jugglery; but in the place of
these they often set mere juristic meditations, in which, because of
the ambitious point of view, one never comes to a clear point of
departure or goal; and, because of equal evaluation of all existing
factors, one never comes to an energetic emphasis of the points
decisive for the legal character of an object. They are also in-
clined to carry over to scientific forms that fluidity of boundaries
which characterizes life with its transitions and mixed forms;
unthinking, they tear down the bounding walls of concepts, instead of building up each concept placed in its own territory so
that the widened relations of life may find a place in it. In order
to escape the uncomfortable and unavoidable force of the rule,
which always distorts the individual character of single cases
which must be forced under it, they finally dissolve the rule into

its concrete specific cases. They flee from the stiff, unchangeable dogma, which strives to stifle every free movement of legal life, but when, among other things, they substitute for every closer definition of a legal institution a description of its concrete relations, when they satisfy themselves with the observation that, according to circumstances, it may be so or so, and leave everything to the free discretion of the judge, then they forget that law without abstract principles is no longer law. While they hurl at their opponents the epithets "scholasticism," "dogmatism," "schematization," they lay themselves open to the counter charges of "unjuristic," "uncritical," "unsystematic." . . . The pragmatic tendency takes its stand more thoroughly, but in a quite different sense from its opponent, upon an *historical* basis, since it conceives of the law of the present as a step in historical development, and therefore is as loath to recognize in the ruling concepts and principles of law as in other sorts of concepts and principles of other periods eternal "legal verities." But, however fruitful this point of view may have been for the history of law, it often has merely negative results for the scientific formulation of the law of the present. For here too it is easier to destroy traditional concepts and formulae recognized through historical study as outworn, as un-German, as dried up, than it is to bring the still fermenting and developing content of our present legal consciousness to well-formulated expression in a new, national, well-grounded system of thought. Finally, great is the debt owing to the pragmatic approach for the uncovering of the internal dependence which binds law with the collective content of national culture. But even here it has not kept free of one-sided exaggeration. It may seldom be disregarded that, in spite of all interaction between it and the other elements of national life, law is still a distinct sphere of life with specific content and purpose; that, therefore, even if it *should* harmonize in the end with moral law on the one hand, and economic conditions on the other, its distinction is still insured, inasmuch as it *can* come into conflict with both. Forgetting this relationship, one often proceeds to consider legal norms as nothing but rules of morality plus external compulsion, or legal relations as nothing but legalized economic relations. . . .

Thus *both* of the juristic tendencies discussed lead in their *one-sided* development to dangerous *fallacies*. . . .

. . . . State law particularly is most wanting in a recognized method of juristic treatment. For a short time a purely pragmatic method has dominated here. The science of state law had scarcely emancipated itself from political philosophy on the one hand and from political history on the other; it scarcely made an effort to pick out of the mass of material a compact system of independent *legal* concepts. The basis, nature, and purpose of the state were subjects of philosophizing, but the hard juristic formulation of its concepts was neglected. Public-law relations were exhibited but no effort was made to analyze them juristically. Analogies with other fields of law were produced in masses, but the formal defining of common and distinguishing characteristics was omitted. All possible characteristic of public law were deduced from the nature of the state and induced from the historical past; but in regard to its juristic construction and systematization one was satisfied with a meager borrowing from private law. . . .

The uncertainty and disunity mentioned in the juristic treatment of state law, the vagueness and indecision of the pragmatic approach, the formalistic reaction with its dry, positive results,—all these phenomena are concentrated in state law upon the argument over the *state concept itself*. . . . Here we find questions whose settlement would seem to be prerequisite to any system of state law, but questions which none the less have scarcely been precisely stated, to say nothing of being satisfactorily answered. Is the state a subject or only an object in public law? If it be subject, has it public-law subjectivity standing alone or only against its members? How is its personality, if it has one, to be juristically conceived? Is it juristically valid only as an external principle or also as an internal principle of the state? Such questions meet us unanswered on the very threshold of state law! Here it is the merit of the formalistic approach to have first pushed through to a clear formulation of question and answer, but its answers have been flat, arbitrary, and incompatible with each other. . . .

II.[2]

---

[2] Section II of this article is devoted to detailed discussion of Max Seydel, *Grundzüge einer allgemeinen Staatslehre* (Würzburg, 1873) and Albert van Krieken, *Über die sogenannte organische Staatstheorie; ein Beitrag zur Geschichte des Staatsbegriffs* (Leipzig, 1873). I have not considered it of sufficient general interest and importance to include in this translation.

III.

. . . . In order to reveal in its indestructible outline the fundamental firmly-established by the newer science, upon which henceforth every further development of public law must certainly rest, we must remember above all that in our time the task of resolving in a higher unity two opposing basic tendencies in the conception of the state fell to science as well as practice.

Of these basic tendencies, one has finally accomplished the denial of the factor of *law* in state law, since it proceeded from the exclusive reality of the generality (*Allgemeinheit*) ; the other, destruction of the concept of *state,* since it postulated the exclusive reality of the individual.

The first of these extreme tendencies dominated the classical world, and, with the restoration of classical ideas, has celebrated its resurrection in philosophy, jurisprudence, and politics. According to it, man exists for the state. Only the *generality* has full reality, is simply its own purpose, bears the basis of its existence exclusively in itself. The individual, in the last analysis, exists not for himself, but for the generality. From this point of view arise all those diverse theories of the origin of the state which play upon the basic Aristotelian theme that the whole comes before the parts. By its very nature, the state presents itself as a plainly independent whole with plainly dependent members, a unit through itself, in itself, and by its own will. With this basic conception, it makes no difference *how* the state is represented in other respects, whether it is portrayed as a natural phenomenon, as a divine institution, as sovereign will, as materialized idea, or as self-developing concept. In juristic reference there must at all events be ascribed to it a personality which is not only plainly unitary, but also all-inclusive, so that, for all those relations into which the state enters, a peculiar personality of the individuals united in the state is unthinkable. To be sure, personality may be ascribed to the individuals also, but this is possible only if there is separated out for them a group of individual relations, completely limited by the state sphere, in which the free, individual wills possess sovereign power. Hence it follows for *law,* whose task is the ordering of the relations of wills arising from the community life of persons, that, by definition, it by no means includes the internal organization of the state. For it is only in relation to the individual sphere left free by the state that there exists a plurality of persons whose spheres of will require limitation as opposed to each other; and however otherwise the relation of this structure to the state may be construed, its content is at all events true and genuine law for individual persons. The *state* order of existence must have a character specifically different from this private law, a character which allows but a single sovereign will for itself. However many similarities may seem to exist between public and private law, there is always lacking to public law the distinguishing characteristics which alone make the latter law. For between a plainly unitary personality and its plainly dependent members, between a causal whole and its controlled parts, there can *never* exist a reciprocity of will relationships.

The tendency toward the opposite extreme of the *individualistic* interpretation of the state dominated in medieval Germany and owed to the natural-law school its complete development, with manifold changes of form, in philosophy, jurisprudence, and politics. At the basis of this approach lies the doctrine that the state exists for man. The individual alone has reality, is his own purpose, exists by nature as a unit. The state is simply a means by which the common, but none the less individual interests of all or many individuals can better be realized with united strength. In regard to the origin of the state it follows then that the individual at all events existed *before* the state, whether the state be considered to have arisen from a more or less consciously creative act of previously disunited individuals, from a more or less free activity of human will, a more or less definite compact or act of subjugation. By its nature, the state presents itself here simply as a complex of persons and institutions (*Einrichtungen*) which work together for a single purpose like the parts of a complicated machine. But this state does not possess an original unity of nature inherent in itself. Even in juristic relations, it is only the individuals who form the state that are possessed of their own original personality. The state as such is *per se* not a person, but a sum of individual persons in unequal positions, some ruling, others ruled. Still while some, driving the implications of individualism to the extreme, simply deny the personality of the state and substitute for it the ruling individuals, others seek, without utterly deserting the individualistic basis, to ascribe to the state, on the ground of external purposiveness, the *role* of a unified subject of law. Also the assumption of juristic personality for the state by no means implies a special characteristic, but merely that a *fiction* is postulated for a technically-formal purpose. This state personality is merely an artificial makeshift, an aid for construction, an abstract creation of thought without reality. It is simply a unity existing in the idea, upon which are bestowed those qualities of an individual needed for the purpose of personification. And so, in fact, not even here is the individualistic basis abandoned, but there is placed beside the natural individual an artificial state-individual. But for *law* there follows from this individualistic concept of the state the possibility of including in equal manner state as well as individual relationships. For the delimitation from each other of independent spheres of will is also related to the ordering of political existence, when this existence is regarded as the result of the interaction of individuals. But, on this basis, public law must finally be construed just as individualistically as private law, and no matter how thoroughly it be veiled, every theory of public law based simply upon the individual must result in a private-law conception. Here, then, in so far as other elements do not oppose it, a complete *legal* character is saved for public law, but this is accomplished only inasmuch and in so far as public law is brought under the idea of *private* law. And what *legal* theory stands to win thereby, *political* theory unquestionably loses.

These opposing basic points of view have, to be sure, seldom been realized in full purity in science any more than in life. . . . But an inner reconciliation and true fusion of the two tendencies could not be accomplished, however close the attempts from both sides may have come, before there had been found a point of departure for public law, which brought into unity the former opposing basic conceptions of the previously antagonistic tendencies. In the discovery of new fundamental principles of this sort, principles which form the kernel of *modern state life* as opposed to that of both classical and medieval periods, lies the greatest achievement of the *modern German science of public law*. An achievement, to be sure, which has scarcely been brought to clear consciousness, which is in many ways concealed and clouded and even now scarcely set at its true value,—but still an achievement which is the basis and the guarantee of all progress in public law.

We proceed from the firmly-established historical fact that man everywhere and at all times bears within himself the double character of existing as an individual in himself and as a member of a collective association. Neither of these characteristics without the other would have made human beings human beings. Neither the particularity of the individual nor his membership in the generality can be thought away without denying the nature of man. Thus we not only accept it as a naturally established fact, but set it down as a conceptual characteristic of man that he has his existence partly in himself alone and partly in an association standing above him. In agreement with this, we assert as well founded a twofold tendency of human consciousness and instinct. Man can have no self-consciousness without *at the same time* recognizing himself as a particular and as a part of a generality. His will receives content and direction only partly from himself; he is also partly determined by other wills. And in so far as we attribute purpose to existence, individual human life is neither mere self-purpose nor a mere means for the demands of the association; but we believe that the individual and the generality exist for themselves and at the same time for each other, and that the task of mankind lies in the establishing of harmony between the mutually complementary factors of the particular and the generality.

From this point of view we must attribute to the human individual as well as to the human association full *reality* and a *unitary character*. For us, the individual existing for himself alone and drawing upon himself is a natural and real life-unit. But we find just as natural and just as real a unity of life in every human association which, by partially absorbing their individuality, binds a group of individuals together into a new and independent whole. For the significance of human existence could as little be created by a mere totaling of the lives (*Lebensinhalt*) of all individuals as it could be expressed by the picking out of single elements of associational life. Thus we find, above the level of individual existence, a second, independent level of existence of human collective associations. Above the individual spirit, the individual will, the individual consciousness, we recognize in thousandfold expressions of life the real existence of common spirit, common will, and common consciousness. And not figuratively, but in the most real sense of the word, we speak of "communities" ("*Gemeinwesen*") over single individuals.

But human communal life is by no means concentrated in a single form everywhere the same, but manifests itself in a rich complex of diverse living structures, continually developing with the progress of culture. Above the narrow and simple communal organizations of older stages of culture, appear continually higher, more inclusive and complete associations, while the narrower associations whose sphere of life is restricted do not thereby lose their lives. Moreover human communal life is continually dividing and branching out according to content and purpose. Originally the purely physical associations, the family, race, nation, fulfilled the whole task of human communal existence. They realized at the same time in unitary and exclusive manner community of speech, morality, belief, economics, laws, and political life. But more and more, in the course of time, the unitary associational organisms split up into a great number of independent associational organisms, each of which dealt with only a single side of human communal life. Although originally these specialized associations simply grew up unconsciously and spontaneously upon a physical basis, the human spirit, when developed to the point, undertook the conscious and deliberate creation of related associations for definite purposes extending beyond the lives of individuals. Corresponding to this development of associational organisms, however, there is also a process of dissolution, of exhaustion, and destruction of creative activity. If the creation of associations is always and everywhere to be conceived as a living stream, then there must also be found always and everywhere, side by side with the perfected associational units, numerous incomplete or degenerate communal structures, mere embryos or dead relics, incomplete and undeveloped attempts, doubtful transitional and intermediate forms of every sort. Moreover, the various associational organisms can overlap and be built upon each other in unbelievable variety; can tie together loosely or closely; can ramify from a common stalk or grow together from different stalks. And so the world of human associational life offers a picture just as colored, variously graduated and organized as the world of organic creatures. In the latter also, the highest and lowest structures have an endless variety of functions and meanings, but common to them all is the characteristic of life. Here also the boundary between embryo and developed individual, even between life and death, is fluid; but the reality of life is not thereby impugned. Here also a bridge of dubious transitional forms leads into the realm of non-organic structures; but the peculiar character of the perfected organism, the ability to construct an independent unity of life, still remains fixed. Finally, here also it is often doubtful where, with the division of an organism, the existence of separate individuals begins, and where, with the coalescing of single creatures, the existence of an organic whole begins; but a unitary nature still remains for us a natural characteristic of an organism.

Among the human associational beings there now belongs particularly the *state*. The nature of the "state" union is to be found in the fact that it has as its purpose the carrying out authoritatively (*machtvolle*) of the common will. It is the association of political action. Its substance is the general *will*, its manifestation is organized *authority* (*Macht*), its function purposive *action*. Political associational life of this sort has always existed; but one speaks of a true state only when an original and distinct organism for state life appears. The isolated tribe, the roaming horde, the wandering clan fulfill state functions, to be sure, but here the state has not yet achieved independent existence. When the latter occurs, political functions can be undertaken by numerous narrower and wider organizations, by graduated political *Gemeinde,* corporations, and unions. They are all of state nature. But *that one* authoritative union (*Machtverband*) whose authority from above is limited by no similar authority, and from below is superior to all similar authority, must exhibit a specific character, and a set of qualitative differences from all other political organizations. For an authority which is the *highest* distinguishes itself from every other authority by the specific characteristic, that it is, through and through, authority (*Macht*) that is simply authority; and a will that corresponds to such authority is distinguished from every other will, as a sovereign, simply general, will, determined by itself alone. For this reason, among the political organizations, although they are all *state-like* (*staatlich*) only the actually highest power-organization may be termed *"state."*

Thus the state is the realization of a definite characteristic side of human communal life. Whereupon it follows in regard to the *origin* of the state, that it is inborn in man to live a state life, and thence that the state is, *generally* speaking, as old as the individual. And also the *separate* state is no free creation of the individual, but the necessary product of social forces active in the individual. States originally came into being and grew without the aid of a conscious creative will,—a natural proof of an unconscious associational instinct. Later, to be sure, they were deliberately and intentionally created, and may even have been founded by a conscious act of will; but even then it is not a collection of individual wills, but the creative act of a general will which calls the state or the new state form into existence. There are no individuals who are simply individuals; no free, unbound, unhypothetical single wills, which could produce from the sum of their individualities the state will through self-restriction and self-renunciation. It would be better to say that these humans, stateless for the moment, who are represented as founders of a state, were always bound together politically in their thought and will, and lacked only momentarily the outward realization of their state existence. Neither the idea of the state nor the determination to realize it could, therefore, have had its roots in the individual spirit; here also, the single active will does not appear as such, but as an element of the common will; and what we see is not a uniting of the wills of many individuals, but a unitary act of the general will residing in many individuals and formless only for the moment, which confirms its own existence and creates for it a form.

As to the *nature* of the state in general, we must, in accordance with what has been said, ascribe to it an *original, real essence.* It appears to us as a human collective organism with a unitary collective life distinct from the life of its members. To be sure, since the state is a *generality,* it arises from other entities which form in it a particular reality; as an associational organism of numerous partly simple, partly associated organisms, it is composed of men and of narrower associations; its life appears in the living activity of members and organs which at the same time lead a separate

existence. But in spite of this it is a real *unity,* because all of
the particular structures, in so far as they are elements of the
state, arrange, relate, and bind themselves in accordance with the
idea of the state whole, and find a content for their being not in
themselves but in their significance for the higher collective life.
If one wished to deny the unity of the state because of its composite nature, this could only be possible in the same spirit and
sense in which one must consider atoms alone as unities and the
world as simply a multiple sum of such unities!

But, since human existence is not exhausted in associational
life, but is at the same time purpose for itself, we must recognize
over against the state the *individual* as an *original* reality, existing for himself and bearing a purpose within himself. For it is
only with part of his being that the single man belongs to the
state as a member; the rest of his being remains completely un-
touched by the communal life of the state, and is the stuff of
his free individuality. Thus state and individual existence stand
side by side as two independent spheres of life, of which neither,
to be sure, can exist without the other and each points toward the
other as its complement, but both of which, for all that, have their
immediate purpose in themselves.

Finally, the state is, of course, generality (*Allgemeinheit*),
but it is by no means, as a widely published doctrine teaches,
simply human society. It is only *one* among the associational organisms of mankind, and only one definite side of human social
life is represented by it. It is possible, to be sure, that, with a
particular people and at a particular time, the state should take
over all or a large number of the functions of social life; but in
higher stages of culture and in the modern world above all, the
non-political sides of human associational life find expression in
special institutions which are in no way to be confused with the
state organization. Although the physical associations of blood,
speech, and habitation are to a certain degree the undeniable basis
for the growth of the state, they can theoretically exist as easily
without the state as the state can exist without them. And even
when the state approaches its ideal of becoming the political organ
of a single and united people, still the natural and political concepts of a people can not be fully amalgamated. Thus the communal life of a people creates for the political as for all other as-

sociation the most important, but by no means the only natural
center. There still exist below the united people (*Volkseinheit*)
the race, the *Gemeinde,* and the family, above it the international
community of culture-peoples, and finally mankind in general, as
narrower and wider human associational institutions with special spheres of life. And so far as a political organization corresponds to these narrower and wider associations they can, on
the one hand, possess a certain independence as against the state,
and, on the other hand, they can, like the state, theoretically divest
themselves of their natural corollary. Furthermore, the ethical-
social, the religious, the artistic and literary, the economic communal experiences all create, at different levels, their own special organisms, all of which have an independent existence as opposed to the state, whether they develop naturally or are consciously directed, whether they are formally proclaimed as unities
or exist only as latent forces, whether they are as permanent as
the church or as ephemeral as many clubs. But if, in the face of
such a wealth of non-state social life, the state must abandon
the pretension of being simple human society, it is indeed still
simply society for those social relations the realization of which
constitutes its nature. And thus, in so far as it deals with common *relations of authority* (*gemeinheitliche Machtverhältnisse*),
all other collective realities, even when they are for their own
spheres political institutions with their own spheres of authority,
are in relation to the state only particular institutions whose
political authority is in the last instance ordered by and subordin-
ated to the authority of the state. Thus, indeed, the living *political*
element of all other social as individual entities finds its final definition of purpose and definitive boundary in the state, which, as
the sovereign organism of social authority, alone among all organisms has no institution above it to limit its power, which, as the
political whole, is alone not a part of another political whole. To
be sure, the question of how far the domain of the state reaches
is not one to be fixed for all time, but depends upon the positive
separation by time and circumstances of the political functions of
life from the other social functions of life. But, in some way or
other, the problems and competence of political authority will
always project themselves into *every* sphere of human social life.
For in general the consideration of how far a general interest re-

quires for its realization the authoritative (*machtvolle*) carrying out of the general will will always be decisive in bounding the political sphere. But to a certain point in all periods and in all cultural environments, all social functions, in order to develop fully' and without hindrance, will be assigned to the protection and care of a power capable of coercing opposing wills. And so the state, even though theoretically it includes but one specific side of social life, is, according to its reason for existence, not an organization founded for a specific single purpose, but its functions correspond with the cultural functions of human society (*Gattung*), because and in so far as a highest power (*Macht*) must exist for their realization. . . .

The nature of law rests in the fact that it *sanctions and defines the external dominion of will within human society.* As soon as a plurality of wills strives for realization, this sort of legal organization is necessary. To be sure, there is another social factor which serves as a norm for will and prevents its ruthless realization. This is *morality*. But morality determines will only from *within*; it appeals to the conscience of the individual and plants therein the notion of *should* (*Sollen*); it aims at the harmony of will with man's own spiritual nature. But social life could not exist without having *externally* as well a norm limiting concurring wills; beside the notion of moral *should* appears the notion that in social relations there is also an external *may* (*Dürfen*) and an external *must* (*Müssen*); there must be not only a harmony of the will with itself, but also a harmony of all wills with one another. Thus arises the idea of *law*—whose final criterion, whether something is ethically or legally in order, resides simply in the conception by which the general consciousness is governed in regard to the setting of norms for the wills in question. Law manifests itself in objective relations as a sum of *norms*, in subjective relations as a sum of *powers* and *duties*. As norm it is an external ruling organization for the wills which it comes upon; as subjective right it is the outward realization of freedom of will, for which a sphere of activity is opened through the powers at the same time that a sphere of obligation is laid upon it by the duties.

The relation of law and state means then simply this: that, on the one hand, law is a particular and unique side of human social life, and, on the other hand, that it is as little possible for law to realize itself without the state as for the state to realize itself without law. We are dealing here, as everywhere else, with all functions of human social life, each of which has its own char· acter and its own roots, and yet each of which is conditioned and determined somehow or other by all the rest, so that only all of them in their collectivity can make up a full human social existence. But between state and law relàtions of reciprocity are of a remarkably close and intimate nature.

This relationship comes to light even in regard to the *origin* of law and state. Law is of equal birth with the state. It is as little drawn from the state as the state from it. But both, springing from independent roots, have developed together, to realize themselves only *through* each other. Like the idea of the state, the idea of law is, generally speaking, born with man. Positive law, however, is the form which any social spirit, but particularly a *Volksgeist,* lends to this original idea. Hereupon, the developed *Volksgeist* makes use of the state to an exceptional degree as the organ for its formulation. But the state does not thereby become either the final source of law nor its only formulating organ. The final source of all law remains the *social consciousness* of any social institution whatever (*Letzte Quelle alles Rechts vielmehr bleibt das* Gemeinbewusstsein *irgend einer socialen Existenz*). The social conviction that something is right needs, to be sure, embodiment through a social declaration in order to come into objective existence as a principle of law. But this declaration can take place in different ways. Usually, of course, it takes place through the state; it is a chief function of the *Kulturstaat* to formulate as law the consciousness of right of the people, and in many periods almost all other sources of law are suppressed by state law. Still beside the state operate in a similar and at times very far-reaching fashion other social organisms—for example, church, family, *Gemeinde,* and so forth—as formative organs of law. And then there still remains in force, in addition to legislation and decree, the informal creation of law through custom, which originally prevailed throughout. In custom the common conviction of right comes to expression and thereby into objective existence as a doctrine of law through the direct activity of respective circles of associations in the life of law. Just at this point two things become clear. In the first place, it appears that there are, indeed, two different spiritual forces of mankind shaping state and law. For the state is the product of the general *will*; law, however, is the outcome of the general *consciousness*. To be sure, reflecting consciousness also works indirectly in the formation of the state, the more the unconscious instinct of will is restricted by conscious decisions of will; and, on the other hand, the organized common will plays the role of an intermediary in the formation of law, the more the cloudy feeling of right gives way to a clear conviction of right. But, nevertheless, the essence of each remains: of the one, embodied will; of the other, embodied conviction. In the second place, it becomes clear that, from a subjective point of view, different categories of associations can be bearers of legal or political life. And so a politically disunited people can maintain the unity of their legal system; and within a single people can exist numerous special categories of law not necessarily coinciding with the political organization. And from the international community of nations, although it lacks state character, can arise international law.

We encounter the same relation of state and law in their *daily activities,* which are separate but still belong together. The life of the state and the life of law are two distinct and specifically different sides of human social life. The former manifests itself in the forceful (*machtvolle*) carrying out of common purpose, and culminates in the political *deed*; the latter shows itself in the marking out of spheres of activity for the wills which it binds together, and culminates in the *recognition* of right. . . . While *force* (*Macht*) is a theoretical assumption for the state, so that a state without every means of force would no longer be a state, it is irrelevant for the concept of law whether it has objective means of force at its command. Law, with or without means of enforcement, still remains *law.* But, however different the social functions of state and law may be, still they are mutually related and can find realization only through each other. The state, to realize its internal strength through the accomplishment of its cultural mission, needs the support of legal concepts; were it accepted simply as active force which, because it has the physical power, claims and finds obedience for every act of will which it considers purposeful, then all political life would freeze into despotism; so the healthy state seeks to base its power upon law, so that the fact of a specific ruling organization will also be accepted as a doctrine of law by the general consciousness of the people (*Volksbewusstsein*), from which there follow self-imposed limitations of political power and corresponding legal obligations of the state. On the other hand, in order to achieve its goal of organized social life, law needs the compensating aid of the state; as the example of international law shows, it can not, without the aid of state power, completely realize its function, but remains incomplete, imperfect law; thus law can only come to its own when the state places its force at its service, establishes courts for its clarification, and forcefully brings each will in conflict with right back to obedience in accordance with the norm.

Thus the *tasks* which state and law have to perform in human life are in no way identical. For the duties of the state are not created by sanction of law, nor the duties of law by the organization of the state; and while the state should advance the social purpose of mankind in every sphere of social life, law has only to mark off the boundaries within which the free pursuit by all existing wills of individual as of associational goals may take place. But, nevertheless, a substantial part of the duty of the state lies in law, and a substantial part of the duty of law, in the state. For, on the one hand, it is an unavoidable and theoretically necessary function of law to order and maintain the internal life of the state. To be sure, history has presented all sorts of variations of this normal relation of state and law. In the Germanic Middle Ages the state was reduced to the position of a mere institution of law, appeared as simply the product and instrument of law, was exhausted in a sum of legal functions; and examples are closer to us in which law does not extend to the state, but is degraded to the position of a pure contrivance of necessity for state purposes. But such one-sidedness in theory has disappeared from modern life and can not be reawakened by any attempts at new theoretical formulations. Theoretically, the *independence* of the idea of the state and of the idea of law in their relation to each other remains fixed for us, however much reality may fall short of theory. The state of the present is for us *Kulturstaat* because it does not restrict itself to the preservation of law, but strives for the perfection of human society on *every* side; but it is at the same time

Rechtsstaat because it stands not outside but *within* the law, and voluntarily recognizes the legal system, in which it sees the result of a concept of equal rank, as a norm for, and limitation upon, its sovereign will.

This fixed independence of the two concepts, basic for our science, leads us back to our starting-point. For the one-sided-ness which wishes either to deduce the concept of law from the concept of the state, or the concept of the state from the concept of law, comes as a consequence of a general conception of human society which is one-sided either in the direction of universalism or individualism. And just as decidedly every scientific theory which proceeds from this sort of one-sidedness appears to us, in spite of its apparent simplicity and misleading formal exact-ness, as an error, not rooted in the present, but in outworn pe-riods of one-sided development. We can expect real progress only upon the basis of a point of view which, however it may otherwise refine itself, proceeds from the independent existence of the whole as of the individual and develops the concepts of law and of the state independently of each other from their independent roots in human nature. We shall be forced, therefore, in spite of all new or newest constructions, to hold firmly to this point of view, as it, in fact, lies at the basis of the ruling theory of public law, though often clouded and obscure.

According to this concept, *state law* is that part of the legal system whose object is the providing of norms for the wills united into a state being. State-law theory is a part of *state theory,* since it deals with one essential side of the state; but it does not create state theory, since the physical, ethical, economic, political nature of the state may be a subject of examination aside from the legal nature of the state, or the purposiveness of political action may be discussed aside from legality. State-law theory is, further, a part of *legal theory,* since it deals only with true and real law; but it does not create legal theory, because law deals also with relations which are not directly connected with the state.

Upon closer observation, state law appears the most important and most characteristic part of *public law,* the antithesis of which is *private law.*

The division of all law into *public* and *private* law appears from the above as a fundamental and creative division. For if law is an ordering (*Normirung*) of spheres of will, human will appears from the beginning in double concept and embodiment as individual will and common will; and so law must bear a specifically different character according to whether, as private law, it limits individual freedom of will, or, as public law, orders the common domain of will. . . .

. . . . Private law sets up individuals as centers of individual spheres of will, and sets up associations, in so far as these move in the circle of relations systematized by private law, as equivalent to individuals. For private law, then, all these individuals are not organized into any higher unity of associational persons. And in private law, of course, individuals are not portrayed as completely unrelated, as isolated atoms, as lawless and dutiless bearers of wills, but their relations to each other are always thought of as mechanical attachments between closed units of life; their possible legal capacities and obligations appear not as an outcome of their membership in a whole, but as variations, expansions, and limitations of their spheres of individuality. The kernel of private law is, indeed, the setting up of a free sphere of activity in which the individual through his own free act of will creates legal relations. . . .

Public law knows no isolated individuals, but only groups and members of groups. Instead of a world of coordinated and self-encompassed units of will, it postulates a world of social beings, in which, from the beginning, will is determined by its organic relations to other wills, in which the composite unity of the whole is referred to the multiplicity of single wills and the multiplicity of single units referred to the unity of the general will, in which, through the simultaneous recognition of the common personality of the whole, and the member-personality of the individuals, there is set up immediately a qualitative gradation of legal entities, a twofold system of will. Public law also creates a sphere of activity for the free will, within which it can work upon the creation of legal relation, but it hereby restricts the will to the limits of the organic position in which it is placed once and for all by the public organization, and its real substance lies in the fixed fabric of norms which constitute the common organism. . . .

The theoretical boundary between private law and public law is in reality fluid, and can, therefore, be fixed at different points by positive law, which must draw the line somewhere. . . .

But in all circumstances and for all time, there is one sphere of law which is simply, absolutely, and for all purposes *public law,* and which is, therefore, the true type of public law and the diametric opposite of private law. This is *state law.* For state law is that law which includes the state as generality and all individuals and other groups as members of the state. From no point of view can this law be regarded as individual law, since there exists no legally organized generality for which the state could be a mere particular. State law is, therefore, different from all other public associational law in the same manner as the state itself differs from other collective entities. In so far as the specific nature of the state as a sovereign institution comes under consideration, there must be set forth a special interpretation of every concept and institution. But, as the state always remains simply the highest among human associations and similar to them in the general characteristics of an associational organism, so state law has a position at the peak, to be sure, but within the general system of public associational law. For this reason, all state-law concepts may be viewed as enlargements of corresponding corporation concepts, and the internal structure of state law is analogous to that of corporation law. Therefore there belongs to the totality of public law a system of thought which repeats itself in very unequal fullness and significance from the lowest steps of organic union up to the state, and to this system there is opposed the private-law system of thought as a closed unit.

The system of public-law concepts must, therefore, separate at the start from the system of private-law concepts, because, while private law deals only with the *external* life of persons, state law, like corporation law, sets norms for the *inner* life of the collective personality. Private law postulates a sum of complete and embodied wills, introduces them as persons, and regulates their external spheres of control. Here, on the other hand, the creation and personification of will is itself the object of the system of law, and the will-relations within an articulated sphere of will are legally regulated. To be sure, the *whole* internal life of the state or of any other associational-organism can by no means be comprehended by law, yet it is *only* law which governs the relation of the many to the one and the continuation of many in the one. But, in so far as it deals with the rule of will (*Willensherrschaft*) and the binding of will (*Willensgebundenheit*), the inner organization of an association is a legal organization; and in so far as the natural, ethical, historic, economic, and social unity of a group indicates also a *legal* unity, a *person,* and in so far as the continuation of the particularity of its parts has not only natural, ethical, and social, but also *legal* significance, *principles of law* govern the relation of the one to the many in an organic whole. . . .

. . . . The real, living *substratum* of an association will always be a *collectivity of persons,* and from this grows the . . . task for public law of regulating personal membership in the association. Specifically, state law will set forth the juristic concept of a national *people.* Thereby it will, in the first place, fix and bound nationality in its external relations. In the second place, however, it must draw the boundary between that part of personality which is incorporated in the state organism through nationality, and that part of personality which remains free whether for the right of the individual or for activity as a member of another association. Here we find the roots of the principle of individual and corporative basic rights or rights of liberty, which not only guarantees to the individual and to other associations a certain sphere not to be disturbed by the state, but also guarantees a sphere of rights which are simply not to be touched by the state.

State nationality as such, like membership in every corporate association, is, on this basis, characterized as a specially created personal *right,* legally acquired and lost. . . . If the conception prevails that the concept of state nationality means only a *passive* sharing in the life of the state, there arises the concept of *subject status;* if on the contrary, *active* participation in the affairs of the state is found in the idea of nationality, then the concept becomes one of the *right of state citizenship.* . . .

Where the idea of subject status has developed, the nationals fall into the roughly divided classes of *rulers* and *ruled.* In such a case, whether the ruler be an individual or a group, the ruler alone is regarded as the bearer of state life; the subjects, on the other hand, will be presented rather like territory as a dead and entirely objective *substratum* of the state body. With the development of the idea of state citizenship, such a point of view is untenable. For when the life of the state throbs in each of its members there can be none who are simply rulers or simply ruled.

On the other hand, it is quite compatible with the concept of the state as an organism living in the whole people that the public system of law should attribute to one or a plurality of all state members a very *predominant* position in the body of the state. Specifically, it lies in the nature of monarchy that one person above all other members of the state has a specific and peculiar significance for the state body. The monarch appears not as an ordinary organ of the state that has simply been appointed by the constitution as a principal organ of state life, but he appears as the *head* of the state body, as a member especially qualified from the beginning, and simply through his intrinsic nature called to this prominent activity for the people. While public law defines and limits this position of the monarch, it attributes to him an original right in the state which is suitable to a highly intensified member-personality within the collective personality. If, in conformity with the usage of history, this law of the monarch is designated as royal *sovereignty,* there is nothing against such designation so long as it remains clear that this sovereignty (so far as it is not simply representation of state sovereignty) has its basis not in opposition to state or law, but simply in opposition to the other members of the state. Since the right to the throne is not something like a right of office, like the right of the highest official in a free state, but an *original* (*eigenes*) right in somewhat the same sense as a civil right or a class right, it also must be considered in the system of state law among the basic elements of the state body, and may not be transferred into the theory of the organization of the state. . . .

Important above all, finally, is the relation of the *corporative* members of the state body, for which arises again a new group of peculiar legal relations unknown to private law. In so far as a corporation is considered generally or for certain purposes as only a special entity as opposed to the state, its public-law position in the state will be equal or analogous to that of single citizens. But special legal relations enter in so far as a corporation is considered as a more restricted community for the state—as an *intermediate organism* between the state-whole and single citizens.

For here it becomes necessary to draw the line between the two capacities of the narrower association—that of being an entity for itself and that of being a member of the state, so it becomes necessary with such an association to distinguish not only between the private-law and public-law sides of personality, but further, within the public-law sphere, between the collective significance of this personality for itself and its significance as a member of the state. So far as the member-position of the narrower association reaches, the state will possess a more or less extended right over not only the external, but also the *internal* life of the organism attached to it. The rise and modification, composition, business, content and compass of membership, its organization and activity in general, will not be determined for the narrower community by its will alone, but to some degree or other by the will of the state. And these legal relations, which repeat themselves in a similar manner in composite corporations, are indeed quite foreign to private law, since it is taken for granted in private law that there can be no right over a person's inner life. . . . It need only be remembered that these corporate members can not only go their own way for different purposes, but can be piled on top of each other for the same purpose; that in the unitary state the whole law of the *Gemeinde,* and of communal and provincial communities of a higher and lower grade, belongs to those basic principles decisive for the elementary composition of the state; finally, that even the federal union of single states into a collective state appears as simply a development of the same idea, and can, therefore, find its theoretical distinction from the decentralized unitary state as well as from the international law *Staatenbund* only from the point of view of a different articulation of its collective personality. . . .

The idea of a *legal organization* and from that the idea of a constitutional law is again common to state law and to all corporation law, but again without analogy in private law. Private law has neither the need nor the possibility of regulating the development of a unity of will in the individual and of examining in its single acts of will the orderly creation of a unitary result out of a multiplicity of elements. . . .

. . . . In the social organism the creation and activity of the organs . . . are to a definite degree objects of law. And so there appears here the *legal concept,* again entirely foreign to private law, of an *organ* as a member of the collective personality constitutionally assigned to a particular function in the life of the community. This concept of a common organ has nothing at all in common with the private-law concept of representative, trustee, attorney, and so forth,—in short, of a person acting for another person,—but the collective personality wills and acts through its organ. It is the unity of the whole itself, the indivisible social person, which acts in law as a living creature whenever the constitutionally authorized organ functions constitutionally. . . .

From this review it appears that, as observed above, the system of state-law concepts is *specifically* different from the system of private-law concepts, while in the system of corporation concepts is found an analogy on a smaller scale. Nothing can be more misleading than to wish to base a system of state law on a differentiation of public functions according to their subjects in helpless dependence on an imitation of the Pandects system, as *Seydel* attempts to do! Every sound system will, on the contrary, be obliged to proceed from an original idea not considered in private law, from the legal construction of a community out of single units. How the single association divides public rights and duties may remain undeveloped here. At all events, in a systematic classification, it will not depend upon the formal character of the subjective or objective relationship impressed upon them, but simply upon their position in the general structure of the state organism. . . .

CPSIA information can be obtained
at www.ICGtesting.com
Printed in the USA
LVHW020012080222
710483LV00014B/642